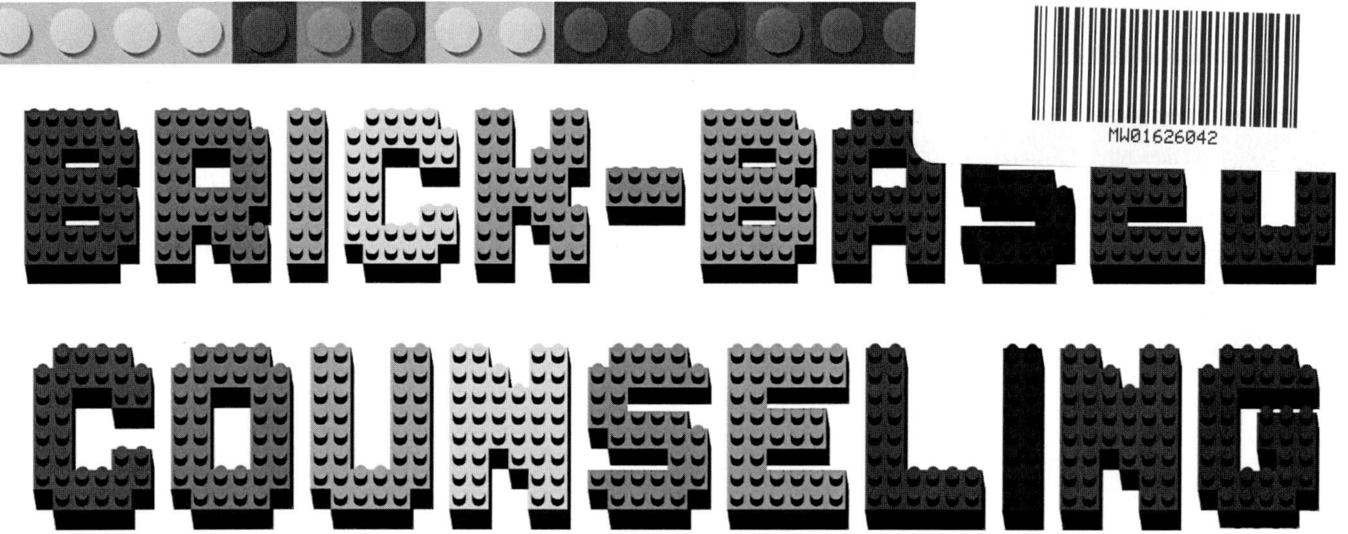

BRICK-BASED COUNSELING

LET'S GET BUILDING!

www.youthlight.com

Cover Design and Layout by Amy Rule

Project Editing by Susan Bowman

ISBN: 978-1-59850-249-7

Library of Congress Number:
2020938594

10 9 8 7 6 5 4 3
Printed in the United States

By Derek Tulluck, M.Ed., NBCT

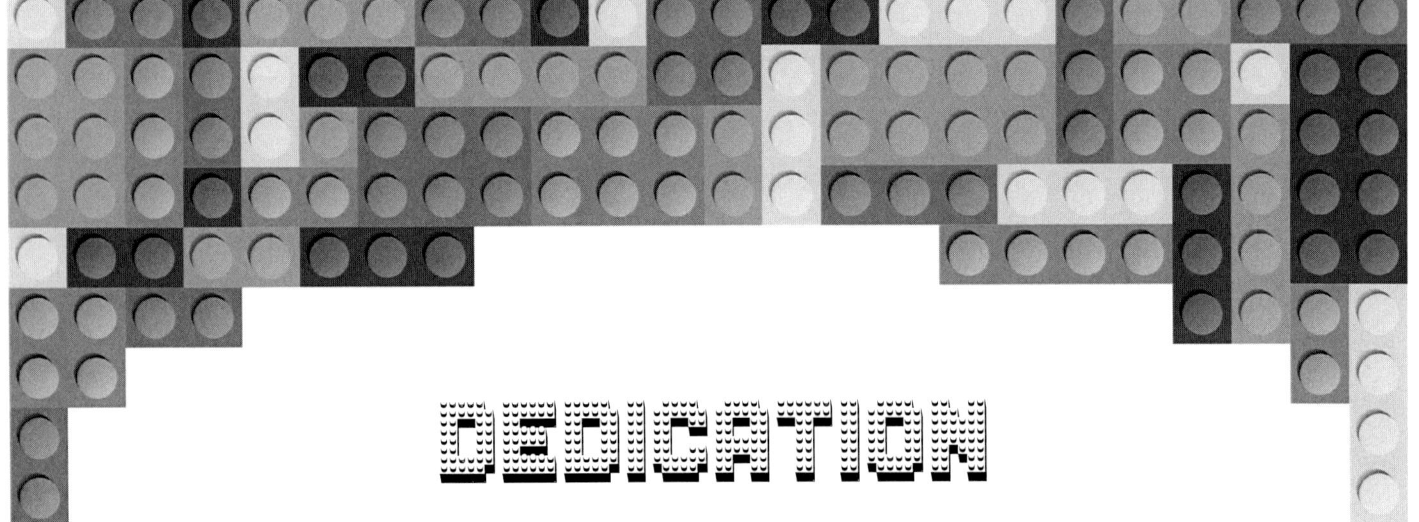

DEDICATION

This book is dedicated to my children Walter and Eliana who remind me each day to find joy in simply taking time to play, and to Aya, my amazing wife for her unwavering support as I spent many hours building with LEGO® bricks and writing this book. I love you all so much.

ACKNOWLEDGEMENTS

I would like to thank Gerrie Garton, for being a wonderful principal, mentor, and friend who helped me grow in so many ways and encouraged me to develop my ideas for using LEGO® in my work with students. Also, I would like to thank my brother Dr. Marco Tulluck, for always inspiring me to dream big and never give up on my goals.

I would also like to say thank you to the YouthLight team for their continued support in guiding me through the process of writing my first book!

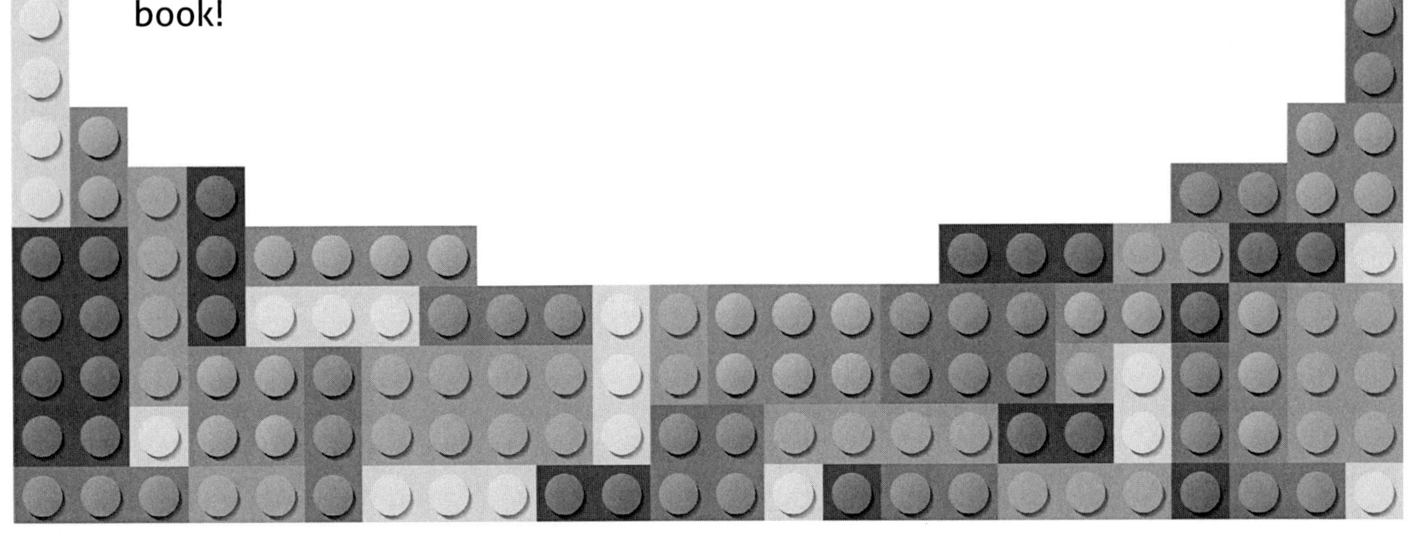

TABLE OF CONTENTS

Introduction 5

Materials and Getting Started 6

Benefits of Using LEGO® Materials 8

Setting Goals and Using Data 11

ART-BASED ACTIVITIES **14**

Section 1: Family and Life Changes (Narrative-Based Approach) 17

1.1 Seasons of Change 18

1.2 Emotion Color Wheel 20

1.3 Ripple Effects of Change 22

1.4 Invasion of the ANTs 24

1.5 Flowers in Bloom 26

1.6 Finding Your Rainbow 28

Section 2: Emotion Management 31

2.1 Rainbow of Emotions 32

2.2 Magic Wand 34

2.3 Brick Bodies 36

2.4 Calm Creations 38

2.5 Gratitude Sculptures 40

2.6 Positive Self-Talk Towers 42

Section 3: Mindfulness 45

3.1 Building in Harmony 46

3.2 Peaceful Patterns 48

3.3 Designs in Nature 50

3.4 Mindful Mirror 52

3.5 Balancing Act 54

3.6 Gardens of the Mind 56

Section 4: Growth Mindset **59**

4.1 Rising Against the Odds 60

4.2 Building on Our Failures 62

4.3 Obstacle Course Challenge 64

4.4 Phoenix Rising 66

4.5 Dream Builders 68

4.6 Keys to Success 70

Section 5: Self-Esteem **73**

5.1 Amazing Animals 74

5.2 Shining Stars 76

5.3 Bricktastic Superheroes 78

5.4 Self-Compassion Build-Ups 80

5.5 Building Your Passion 82

5.6 Building Positive Qualities 84

COLLABORATION-BASED ACTIVITIES **87**

Section 6: Friendship Groups **89**

6.1 Sharing Ideas, Listening, and Making a Plan Together 92

6.2 Sharing, Trading, and Taking Turns 94

6.3 Offering and Asking for Help 96

6.4 Handling Disagreement and Conflict 98

6.5 Respecting Different Perspectives 100

6.6 Giving and Receiving Compliments 103

Sections 7-9: Group Projects on Comic Books/Social Stories, Architecture, & Stop-Motion Animation .... ***Digital Files***

About the Author **105**

References **106**

Digital Files

Online access to the digital files for Sections 7, 8 and 9 are available at youthlight.com. Simply enter the Library of Congress number listed on the copyright page of this book to gain access to all of the available files.

INTRODUCTION

As an elementary school counselor, I am always looking for creative ways to authentically engage students in positive experiences that promote social-emotional learning in a safe, supportive, and accessible way. Over the past several years, I have found that LEGO® materials provide an engaging, versatile, and meaningful tool for working with students in a variety of counseling settings, including individually, in small groups, and classroom lessons. In my professional work with students, I have developed numerous successful strategies for incorporating brick-based activities to support social-emotional, academic, and career development. I am excited to have the opportunity to share these activities with other professionals who may find them beneficial in their work.

This book is intended for school counselors, therapists, educators, and other professionals working with children and provides a variety of brick-based activities that support social-emotional development for use with students or clients in individual, group, or classroom settings. The activities presented in this book address several relevant topics such as emotion management, resilience, problem-solving, positive peer interactions, and growth mindset. These activities are designed primarily for use with students from preschool through 8th grade. In this resource guide, I will be sharing with you several brick-based counseling activities you can use with your students or clients, along with insights I have learned along the way to implement a brick-based counseling approach that is effective and affordable!

Let's get building!

Derek Tulluck, M.Ed., NBCT

MATERIALS AND GETTING STARTED!

(ON A BUDGET!)

In order to start implementing a brick-based program, you of course first need to have access to LEGO® materials. At this point, you might already be asking "but aren't they expensive?" LEGO® materials often have a reputation for being expensive, and there are costly LEGO® sets out there, but you do not need to buy giant sets based on popular movies to begin implementing brick-based counseling activities in your program. You really do not need much at all to get started and most of the activities in this book will require only a basic set of materials. Chances are, you may already have a set you could use. If not, a small, basic tub of LEGO® bricks is really all you need to begin, which can be purchased relatively inexpensively (around $30 US). If cost is a barrier, you can often find used LEGO® bricks in good condition that are reasonably priced, or if you ask around, you could probably even find someone who has some they would be willing to donate. In my experience, donations are often the best way to acquire LEGO® materials.

A great way to look for donations is to start by posting a message on social media to see if anyone has LEGO® bricks they are willing to part with. LEGO® bricks are very popular materials that lots of people already have, and you may be pleasantly surprised to find that you have friends or family who would be happy to pull a tub that's just collecting dust out of the back of their child's closet and free up some space. I have had several people donate LEGO® bricks to me over the years including parents who said their kids had way too many that they never play with and even teachers who were retiring had some they no longer needed. You may also consider writing a grant, such as to your school PTA to help acquire materials to get started. The point is that you don't need to spend a lot of money to start implementing a brick-based program and there are lots of ways you could acquire them at little or no cost.

If you find that you enjoy using LEGO® bricks in your sessions with students or clients, you may decide to invest in more specialized pieces, LEGO® Minifigure characters, or other resources to grow your program. Notice that I intentionally use the word "invest" here. LEGO® materials are built to last and can be reused over and over again, which is invaluable when working with a high number of students or clients. So, if you do decide to expand your collection of materials, it is nice to know that because LEGO® products are built with such excellent quality, they are durable and will likely last for years to come. Much of the materials in my own personal collection have been used multiple times a day for several years by hundreds of elementary school students with virtually no damage or broken pieces. That's what I call reliable.

In addition to regular LEGO® bricks, children are often very interested in using the LEGO® Minifigure characters and accessories. These can be quite costly and certain characters or items may only come with some of the larger or more expensive sets. Fortunately, there are websites where you can order individual characters, specialized pieces, or accessories from sellers internationally at affordable prices. Depending on the topic of the group, lesson, or session you are facilitating, you may find that there are specific pieces that you want to incorporate to enrich the experience. For example, if you are doing an activity with younger children that involves building a fire station and discussing community helpers, you may want to order a couple of extra firefighter characters so there will be enough for each participant in the group to choose a character to use and play with. On occasion, LEGO® pieces can sometimes get lost or go missing, so these websites are also a great resource to affordably replace pieces if needed. Replacement pieces can also be ordered directly through the official LEGO® website as well.

Throughout this book, I will introduce a wide variety of brick-based counseling groups, lessons, and activities that cover many topics or needs. For each activity, I will provide a list of recommended materials, but ultimately you will be able to implement most activities in this book with at least a basic set of LEGO® materials. I suggest that you start small and expand your collection of materials over time as needed. In addition to a basic set of LEGO® materials, you will also need a couple of inexpensive items for storage. Here is a complete checklist of items I recommend for getting started as well as some additional tips to help you stay organized.

Getting Started Checklist

1. Set of LEGO® Materials (A classic set of 484 pieces is sufficient, LEGO® DUPLO® materials are recommended for preschool-aged children)
2. Small Tubs (For students working in pairs and sharing materials during sessions)
3. Resealable Storage Bags (Useful for sorting special pieces or LEGO® Minifigures)
4. LEGO® Minifigures (As needed depending on the type of activities implemented)

Tips for Organizing and Managing LEGO® Materials

1. Use tubs to separate LEGO® pieces. Depending on what you have, you may wish to sort by color or type. This can be useful for locating pieces, but I recommend that you do not sort every single LEGO® piece you have by color. Keep some mixed for general use.
2. Use smaller tubs or trays to provide a manageable amount of bricks for students to use during sessions. Having too many pieces on the table can be overstimulating and can also create a mess that takes time to clean up. During group sessions, assign one tub per student or for each team to share depending on the type of activity.
3. For activities involving LEGO® Minifigure(s), keep characters presorted in resealable storage bags with an index card inside indicating what characters or accessories should be stored in the bag. This keeps items ready to go for different sessions and makes it easier to clean up.
4. Allow each student to typically choose only 1 LEGO® Minifigure character so they do not become lost or go missing. Also, I recommend asking students to please keep their characters together and not remove or switch their heads and body parts because this makes them get mixed up and harder to keep track of.
5. Ensure that all materials are appropriate for your setting. For example, as a school counselor, I remove and dispose of all weapons such as guns or swords that are sometimes included with characters such as police officers or pirates.
6. If you start to collect a large amount of accessories and smaller pieces, a fishing tackle box can be a handy way to keep small pieces organized and readily accessible.

BENEFITS OF USING LEGO® MATERIALS

As an elementary school counselor, small groups are an integral part of my program and I have developed a variety of activities utilizing LEGO® materials to address different needs and create meaningful and engaging group experiences for students of different age levels. Not only are LEGO® bricks fun and appealing to a broad age range, but they can be utilized effectively to support the development of a broad range of social-emotional and academic skills.

As a counselor, here are some of the greatest benefits to incorporating brick-based activities in your work with students.

Student Engagement and Interaction

When I develop group activities, student engagement is always my first priority, and when working with children, I believe a play-based approach often works best. By their very nature, LEGO® bricks are colorful, fun, and full of possibilities. This creates an enjoyable, safe, and accessible environment for both younger and older students or clients. It also encourages hands-on participation and interaction which opens the door for greater communication and makes for a more positive experience overall. I have also found LEGO® building to be a calming activity to help students self-regulate prior to, or during conversations that may be more challenging or emotional for students.

Versatility and Durability

One of the things I appreciate most about LEGO® materials is their versatility in developing activities that are appropriate and engaging for various age levels. With the same collection of LEGO® materials, I can implement developmentally appropriate group activities and projects to meet the needs of Kindergarten students or 5th grade students. The purpose, approach, or complexity of the activity may change depending on the needs of the students, but you can still use the same basic materials regardless of the activity which makes LEGO® materials such a versatile tool for counselors. Additionally, LEGO® materials are built to last and can be used over and over again for numerous years, making them incredibly durable. As a counselor on a budget, not having to replace materials and being able to reuse them year after year is very helpful.

Play and Social-Emotional Development

Through a play-based approach to counseling, the natural and authentic element of play is used as a framework to help children practice valuable skills such as emotion regulation, communication, problem-solving, decision-making, and team collaboration. When students participate in a brick-based counseling session or activity, the elements of play, creativity, and discovery encourage positive interaction among group members and a sense of purpose and empowerment for the participants. The playful nature helps to create a safe and fun environment that also enables you to build rapport with students. This relationship building helps form group cohesiveness and trust, which provides a foundation for meaningful social-emotional growth.

Unfortunately, in today's society, children are experiencing far less opportunities than previous generations to play freely with other children as families become busier and technology has permeated so much of our daily lives, and the consequences are significant. According to researcher Peter Gray in his article *The Decline of Play and the Rise of Psychopathology in Children and Adolescents*, it is through play, children develop essential skills including "how to get along with others, inhibit their impulses, and regulate their emotions" and states that "without play, young people fail to acquire the social and emotional skills necessary for healthy psychological development." As a result of less opportunities for play, children are experiencing a significant need for more social-emotional support which is sadly demonstrated in an increased number of children affected by mental health issues. In fact, "Over the past half century, in the United States and other developed nations, children's free play with other children has declined sharply. Over the same period, anxiety, depression, suicide, feelings of helplessness, and narcissism have increased sharply in children, adolescents, and young adults." (Gray, 2011)

Through incorporating a play-based approach, we provide an authentic setting for students to strengthen underdeveloped social-emotional skills. This can be provided through a combination of self-directed free play that promotes agency and creativity, as well as guided play that offers students opportunities to participate in activities of appropriate rigor, while the counselor provides appropriate scaffolding and modeling as needed to support optimal skill development. Guided play activities can also often be connected directly with social-emotional learning standards and incorporate various assessment strategies to measure progress which will also be discussed in this book. As children engage in play-based social-emotional learning activities as outlined in this book, they receive authentic, in-the-moment feedback and support from the counselor to promote meaningful development of social-emotional skills.

Additionally, play has an important role in overall development. Through play, children build on their ability to use a variety of other skills associated with learning and development. Research from the LEGO® Foundation states that "Learning through play supports overall healthy development, acquisition of both content (e.g., math) and learning-to-learn skills (e.g., executive function)" (Zosh, et al., 2017). By utilizing a play-based approach with LEGO® bricks in counseling groups, we are able to provide students with meaningful opportunities to develop interconnected skills, which will provide a stronger foundation for social-emotional and academic success in the 21st century.

Integrating 21st Century Skills and Project-Based Learning

Through brick-based activities, students experience opportunities to develop essential 21st century skills such as the Four Cs of communication, collaboration, creativity, and critical thinking (Partnership for 21st Century Learning) which are naturally embedded in shared building experiences. Along with these skills, there are also ample opportunities for incorporating technology use and blended learning, as well as various academic skills and content areas, which allows for unique interdisciplinary, project-based learning experiences. One of my favorite groups that I like to implement is an architecture themed group. In this group, students work collaboratively to design and build structures with LEGO® bricks while applying various architectural concepts. The process is a very integrated experience that blends STEAM (Science, Technology, Engineering, Arts and Math), social studies, marketing, technology, project-management, and other skills.

As an example, I gave a group of 5th grade students an assignment to design and build an expansion for Tokyo Disneyland®. Throughout the process, students researched the attractions currently available, developed a map of the layout for their new expansion land, developed themed-attractions, created concept art, built a model with LEGO® bricks, and created marketing materials to promote it. Through it all, they also learned to come together as a team, communicate, handle frustration, resolve conflicts, empathize, respect differences, synthesize ideas, and delegate tasks. Altogether, it was an incredibly rich and enjoyable learning experience that supported social-emotional, academic, and career development in multiple ways.

Promoting a Growth Mindset

Children often make mistakes which can cause strong emotions such as disappointment, frustration, or anger. One of the great things about building and playing with LEGO® materials is that they allow opportunities for mistakes, rebuilding, and continual growth. If a student makes a mistake building something or they are having difficulty, they may sometimes experience strong emotions. These are often wonderful teaching moments in which we can connect with the student, co-regulate emotions, and solve a problem together by taking the LEGO® pieces apart and rebuilding to fix a mistake or work through a challenge. Brick-based activities such as those presented in this book provide valuable learning opportunities that empower young children to learn to persevere through challenges, develop social-emotional skills, and become creative problem solvers. These experiences promote a sense of agency and strong self-efficacy as children experience and learn that they are capable of overcoming challenges, building positive relationships, and achieving success.

SETTING GOALS AND USING DATA

As a school counselor, I typically meet with students for group sessions at a scheduled time on a weekly basis. This usually means that the student will be missing some part of class time and that the teacher may need to catch them up on later. If I am going to be taking a child out of class for 30 minutes to work with them, I believe it is critical that I am clear about how that time is going to be utilized and for what reason. In order to make sure group time is used effectively, I find it very helpful to develop goals to help establish a clear sense of purpose and focus for the activity or work that will be taking place during the group process. This same principle of having a clear purpose is also equally applicable to teaching classroom lessons.

When developing goals, I recommend aligning them with established social-emotional learning (SEL) standards such as the ASCA Mindsets and Behaviors for Student Success. Specific goals can be chosen based on the counselor's knowledge of the students' needs, feedback from teachers or parents, student-selected, or based on other data. Established goals provide a framework that can be referred to during sessions and used for assessment to monitor student growth. Having an established goal provides a common purpose that connects group members. This also helps to provide clear expectations which can reduce behavior management issues or utilizing time ineffectively due to students who are off task and do not know what they should be working on.

There may be several students participating in a single group who all have multiple needs and there may be several different goals that need to be worked on. Depending on what is needed, you may find that establishing one goal for the entire group is best or you may decide to differentiate and work with each participant to develop more individual goals. You could also have both an overall group goal as well as an individual goal for each participant. You can certainly develop other goals that are relevant to particular sessions or for a specific participant, but I recommend that you keep a primary goal that will remain the same throughout the duration of the entire group process that can be referred back to continually and used for data purposes to measure the overall effectiveness of the group.

I find that goals are best written in an easy-to-understand learning target and success criteria style format similar to what many teachers would use in the classroom for math or reading. Rather than using academic standards, we are using standards for social emotional learning. These goals should be written in concise and easy to understand "I can" statements and include usually 2 or 3 success criteria or items that will let participants know that they have met the target. To gain student buy-in, I find it is more effective to dedicate time during the first session to have the participants help determine what the goal and success criteria should be. Once this has been established, I like to print out the goal and briefly review it with the participants at the beginning of every group session to ensure consistency. For example;

ASCA Standard: *SS2. Create positive and supportive relationships with other students*

Learning Target: *I can be a good friend.*

Success Criteria:
1. *Listen to others*
2. *Share the materials*
3. *Solve problems respectfully*

Depending on the age and needs of the participants, there can be significant variation between groups on how the learning target is written or what the success criteria will be. You may also consider differentiating within a group to provide more individualized goals, which can help create a more equitable and meaningful experience for all students, however, you also want to be careful not to create confusion by having too many goals. If you feel there is a need for more individualized goals, I recommend that you create a common overall learning target for the entire group and then modify the success criteria as needed to differentiate for a particular student. The overall goal might be "I can be a good friend," but that could look different depending on what a particular student needs to work on. For example, one student might need to work on using kind words, while another student needs to practice asking politely for something instead of taking it out of someone's hand. The success criteria can be written in numerous ways to meet the specific needs of the students; just make sure to talk with each student about what it means and also consider role-playing or demonstrating the skill to help ensure comprehension and equip them to be successful in reaching their goal.

In order to keep track of student progress on the established learning target or goals for the group, student self-assessment is a strategy that I have found to be successful and recommend implementing as it allows students to truly reflect on their own behavior and decide for themselves what they did well and what they feel they need to work on. I believe this helps encourage participants to develop a growth mindset and internal locus of control which empowers students to take responsibility for their own choices. Research from John Hattie's Visible Learning study also demonstrates that self-assessment is one of the most effective strategies for supporting student growth.

In my experience, students tend to rate themselves highly on self-assessments especially if they can see what the other participants are putting on their papers. To achieve more authentic results, a privacy folder or other strategy might be beneficial. If students rate themselves in a way that you feel does not accurately reflect something, this is a great opportunity for the counselor or facilitator to talk individually with that student to provide an opportunity for them to explain their rationale behind how they rated themselves, or to provide feedback. I utilize a rating-scale format in which students choose a number, word, or symbol to measure their performance. You can choose whatever format works best for your group. Here is an example of self-assessment scale.

Self-Assessment Rating Scale:			
1	**2**	**3**	**4**
Not Yet	**Sometimes**	**Usually**	**Mostly**
😟	🙂	😀	😎

Depending on the needs of your group, you may choose to have students fill out a form to rate how well they believe they are doing overall or you could also go deeper and have them fill out the rating scale for each of the success criteria as well. I find this to be helpful as it allows students an opportunity for greater self-reflection and provides more detailed data about student progress with each of the success criteria. For example, you might see a pattern begin to emerge that the student is rating themselves a 4 in sharing, but a 2 in problem-solving. This data could inform your practice as a counselor in identifying areas of need where a student might need additional support. Here is an example of what a rating scale could look like if you wish to have students self-assess using multiple success criteria:

Learning Target: *I can be a good friend.*				
1. I listened to others.	**1**	**2**	**3**	**4**
2. I shared the materials.	**1**	**2**	**3**	**4**
3. I solved problems respectfully.	**1**	**2**	**3**	**4**

In presenting the self-assessment to the participants, you may prefer to use a new sheet each session, or you can utilize one goal sheet to track progress throughout the duration of the group, which I find to be more convenient. For each group, I use a simple file folder labeled with the name of the group and then keep a goal sheet for each student in the folder. At the end of each group session, you can easily pull out the folder, have students fill out their forms by circling their score with a pencil, and then put them back in the folder so they are ready to use for the next session. Here is a recommended format for a multi-week goal sheet:

Learning Target: *I can be a good friend.*				
	Session 1	**Session 2**	**Session 3**	**Session 4**
1. I listened to others.	**1 2 3 4**	**1 2 3 4**	**1 2 3 4**	**1 2 3 4**
2. I shared the materials.	**1 2 3 4**	**1 2 3 4**	**1 2 3 4**	**1 2 3 4**
3. I solved problems respectfully.	**1 2 3 4**	**1 2 3 4**	**1 2 3 4**	**1 2 3 4**

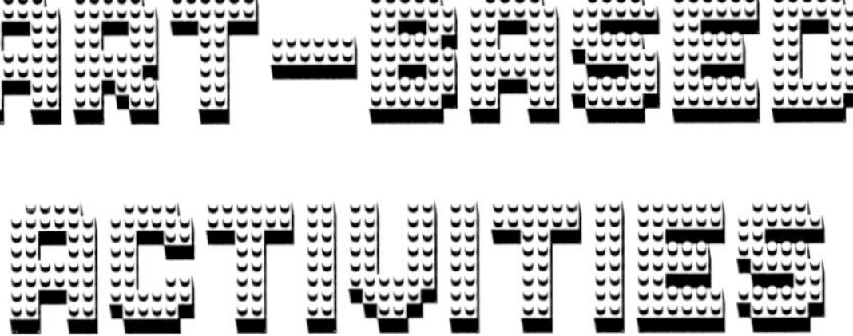

Overview and Topics

Art-based activities are often an inviting and meaningful way to support children who are experiencing significant life events with identifying, expressing, and coping with strong emotions. In recent years, I have been exposed to modern artists who use LEGO® bricks as a medium for their artwork. As a counseling professional with a passion for art therapy and for utilizing LEGO® in my work with students, I was inspired to combine the two. In this section, you will find a variety of brick-based, art activities, which I commonly refer to as "Brick Art." These activities appeal to a broad age-range and are designed to address a variety of counseling topics as listed below.

- Family and Life Changes (Divorce, Grief and Loss, Trauma, Military, etc.)
- Emotion Management
- Mindfulness
- Growth Mindset
- Self-Esteem
- Friendship and Collaboration

Guidelines for Facilitating Art-Based Activities

Art-based activities are designed to help participants identify, explore, and express feelings related to significant life events through art-making using LEGO® bricks and subsequent discussion either individually or in a group setting. I recommend a Narrative approach to facilitating these individual or group sessions in which the belief is that the client is the expert about their own story and the counselor's role is to provide a safe environment for participants to explore and express themselves. During art-based activities, the counselor fulfills the following primary duties:

1. Establish prompts relevant to the group topic or purpose.
2. Provide participants space to work through their thoughts and feelings related to the prompt.
3. Offer encouragement and assistance as needed when participants are working.
4. Ensure an opportunity for each participant to have a voice and share their work and ideas.
5. Engage participants in meaningful discussion with both counselor-led or participant-led discussion questions and compliments.

During these sessions, students will be provided with a prompt and be given time to use the LEGO® materials to independently create and build something that relates to that prompt. These prompts can be concrete or more abstract, but ultimately allow the client the space to tell their own story and express themselves freely. An example prompt for students in a self-esteem group might include "Build something that represents a challenge you have overcome." In response, one student may create a soccer goal and talk about a time when they scored the game-winning goal, and another student might build a piano and discuss a difficult song they learned to play. Group discussion may then center on having the students identify and discuss the personal strengths or character traits that helped them in overcoming those challenges.

As students are working, I find that many students enjoy listening to some relaxing background music as they are building. During this time, I also confer 1-on-1 with each person in the group to ask briefly about what they are building, ask if they need any help with anything, and offer some positive feedback or a compliment about their idea or how they designed their creation. This is not meant to be a test of how well a student can build with LEGO® bricks, so if a student says that they want to build something in particular and are having difficulty, it is totally acceptable for the counselor to help them find pieces that might help them with their project. In fact, these small moments go a long way in building a positive rapport and establishing trust.

Let the students know that they are the artist and encourage them to design and build however they want. Reassure them that it doesn't have to look a certain way and that you are there to support them if they need any assistance. Some students may have an idea of what they want to create but will need support with actually building it. I find that doing an online image search for specific things made out of LEGO® bricks is a great way to offer a model for students to refer to when making their own creations. Offering support like this help us to respond to the needs of the students and provide a safe and equitable environment where everyone can participate and successfully benefit from, and contribute to the group.

As each group session comes to a close, the counselor should make sure that each student has had an opportunity to share and participate in the group discussion. It is also great to end group sessions on a positive note by thanking the students for sharing and offering additional positive feedback or compliments. This helps to build the participants' self-esteem and encourage positive connections between group members as they learn to value and appreciate each other's unique qualities and ideas.

Suggested Outline for 30-Minute Session

1. Welcome and Group Norms
2. Review Goal
3. Introduce Activity
4. Mini-Lesson
5. Activity Work Time
6. Presentations and Compliments
7. Clean up
8. Self-Assessment

*Note on Saving Projects

It's important to note that there is also a potential challenge awaiting at the end of the session as many students will feel a strong sense of pride in what they built and will ask to save their creations and put them on display. At times, it may be possible to put a few items on a shelf and save them for a little while, but inevitably you will run out of space to keep doing this and you will probably find that you need the pieces to complete projects with other groups. To manage this issue, there are 3 solutions that I have found to be effective:

1. Share with students that building with LEGO® bricks is similar to building a sandcastle on the beach and that it won't last forever. I typically allow them to put their item on a shelf in the office somewhere to display it and then I will disassemble it at the end of the day.

2. Create a digital portfolio of their work by taking a picture of each of their builds and then printing it for them at the conclusion of the group. Typically students are comfortable with disassembling their projects once you take a picture of it. Actually creating a portfolio and managing pictures of individual student projects is time consuming, so be mindful about whether or not you can commit to this solution.

3. Enforce a rule that everyone must clean up and put all of the materials away once the timer goes off. Some students have a difficult time with transitioning, and this can turn into a power struggle on occasion. For students that have a hard time cleaning up and moving on, I usually ask them to leave their pieces on the table so they are not late going back to class. If you know certain students need more time to transition, it can be helpful to set a timer before the actual clean-up timer to let them know they have 2 minutes left to finish building before everyone is going to put the materials away.

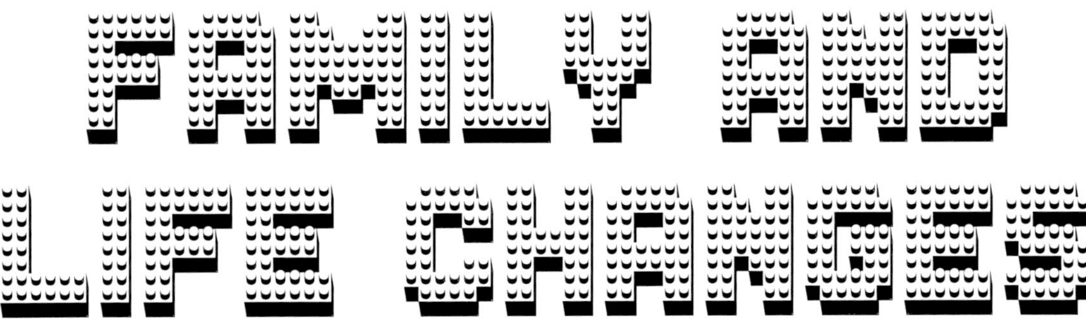

FAMILY AND LIFE CHANGES

(Narrative-Based Approach)

SECTION 1

In this section, you will find a sequence of 6 brick-based art activities to support students with family and life changes. The activities for each session are based on a general narrative counseling approach and are developed to be general enough to be appropriate for a wide range of family or life changes such as divorce, grief, or trauma, or what will be referred to as a "change event" in the following lesson plans. Each activity allows the participants to engage in art-making using LEGO® materials that is representative of their own personal narratives and life circumstances. In the school setting, often there may not be enough students dealing with the same issue at the same time to form a group around one topic. The approach used here provides a versatile framework that enables the counselor to include and provide meaningful support for participants with different life circumstances in the same group, which helps ensure that all students receive needed services.

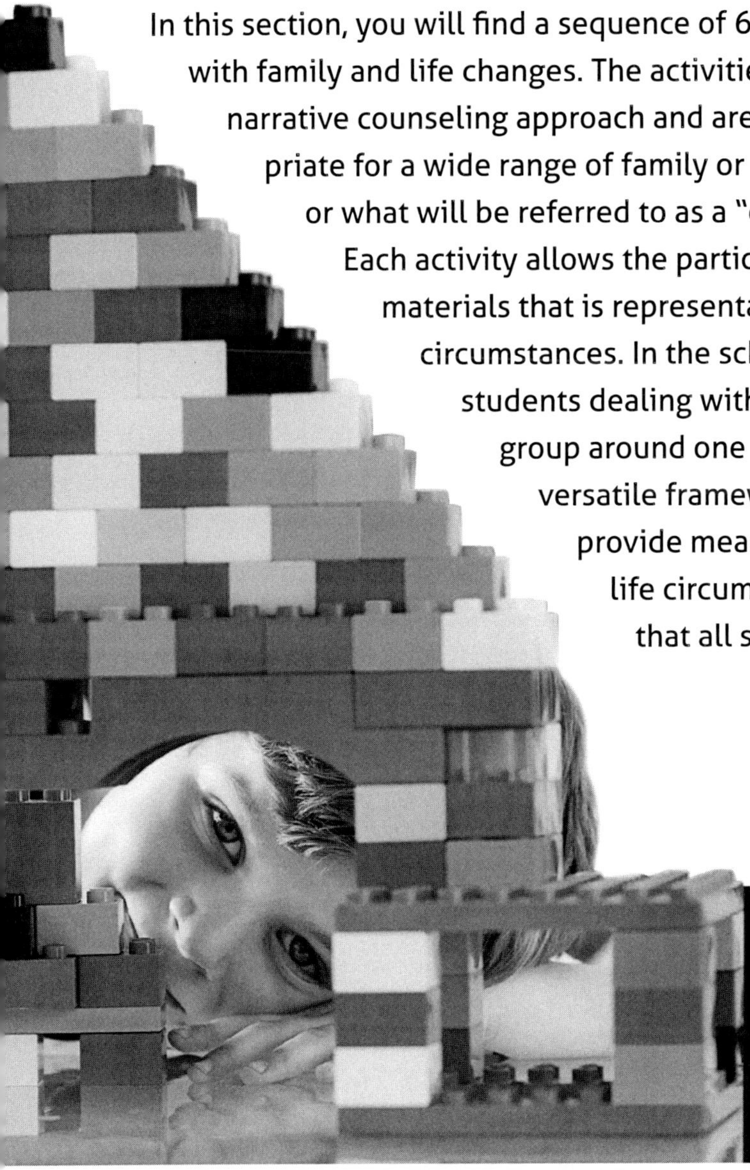

ACTIVITY 1.1

SEASONS OF CHANGE

DESCRIPTION OF ACTIVITY

Students will build a structure that represents the change they are experiencing.

LEARNING OBJECTIVE(S)

- Students will be able to identify and describe a significant life change.
- Students will use their LEGO® structure to assist them in discussing the impact of the identified life change.

PROCEDURES

1. Begin by explaining that each person in the group is here today because we have all experienced some changes and that we are meeting together to provide a safe space for people to share at their comfort level about those changes. I like to start with a brief activity by showing students photos representing the four seasons of Spring, Summer, Fall, and Winter. Discuss with the students what changes happen in each season. Explain that when we go through changes in our lives, it can be like entering a new season and sometimes those seasons bring with them different feelings and events.
2. Next, explain that today we are going to do an activity with LEGO® bricks to help us reflect on our current "season" and the changes we are going through and what we would like to share with the group.
3. To help the participants better understand the activity and what types of things they might consider building, offer some ideas such as a person who recently lost a loved one may create a structure that represents a favorite activity they used to do with that person, such as building an ice cream cone out of LEGO® bricks and sharing about how they really enjoyed going to the ice cream shop with their grandpa before he passed away, or a student could build a LEGO® model of their new house that they moved to after their parents got divorced.
4. Next, remind the students that there is no right or wrong way to do the activity and that they can choose whatever they want to build that is related to the change they have experienced.
5. As students are working, confer with each member of the group regarding what they are making and what they would like to share to describe their change experience. This provides an opportunity to connect with each student and allows each student to rehearse what they would like to say to the whole group when it is time to share and discuss.
6. To help students transition, let them know when it is almost time to share and reassure them that is okay if they did not completely finish what they wanted to build. I suggest you also have students pause for a moment to take a deep breath and make sure they are

calm and ready to share what they made. This activity can be challenging and emotional for some students to build and talk about.

7. Provide each student with the opportunity to share briefly about what they made and the emotions that it represents. Allow each student the opportunity to share at their comfort level. If a student wishes to pass, this should always be an option to ensure a safe environment. Also, let the student know, however, that if they change their mind and want to share, they can. After each student has an opportunity to share, follow up with group discussion using the questions provided below.

Discussion Questions

1. When did you first find out about the change?
2. How do you feel about the change?
3. What has been challenging for you since the change?
4. What has helped you deal with the change?
5. What is something positive that has happened since the change?

Follow-Up or Extension Activities

- Students may build 2 structures that represent their life before the change occurred and after the change.
- Students may build more than one structure if they have multiple changes they are struggling with such as parental divorce, moving to a new school, and not having any new friends.

ACTIVITY 1.2

EMOTION COLOR WHEEL

Description of Activity

Students will build an emotion color wheel and a corresponding LEGO® structure that represents their feelings about the change event.

Learning Objective(s)

- Students will be able to identify emotions they are experiencing and represent them with a corresponding color using LEGO® materials.
- Students will use their LEGO® structure to assist them in describing the identified emotions and how those emotions impact them.

Additional Materials Needed

- Paper
- Markers

Procedures

1. To begin this activity, explain that when changes occur in our lives, we often experience a variety of emotions that can sometime be confusing or overwhelming. Let the students know that we are going to first discuss some different emotions by creating an emotion color wheel with LEGO® bricks. To create the color wheel, place a large piece of paper in the middle of the table and draw a large circle. Have the students each place an individual LEGO® brick of as many colors as they can find around the circle. Then, discuss each color and have the students name as many emotions as they can that they feel are represented by each color. There is no correct answer for this and answers can vary. Some examples could include red = anger, blue = sadness, black = loneliness, orange = anxiety, and so on. Depending on your students, you may wish to have students create their own individual color wheels to encourage more independent reflection about their emotions.

2. Next, explain that today we are going to do an activity with LEGO® bricks to help us explore the emotions we have regarding the change event. Explain that the students will be asked to build a structure out of LEGO® materials that represents the different emotions they have. To represent specific emotions, the students will choose colors that correspond with the emotions listed on the emotions color wheel. This activity intends to help students name and externalize the emotions they are experiencing by creating a physical and creative representation of them.

3. To help the participants better understand the activity and what types of things they might consider building, offer some ideas such as creating a LEGO® structure in the shape of an animal, person, or a certain object that they feel is representative of their emotions

in some way. An example could be a house built out of blue bricks to represent feeling alone and sad at home after the loss of a loved one.

4. Next, remind the students that there is no right or wrong way to do the activity and that they can build anything they want to represent their emotions. The only guideline is that they build their structure using colors that correspond with certain emotions.
5. As students are working, confer with each member of the group regarding what they are making, the emotions represented, and what they would like to share with the group about their work. This provides an opportunity to connect with each student and allows each student to rehearse what they would like to say to the whole group when it is time to share and discuss.
6. To help students transition, let them know when it is almost time to share and reassure them that is okay if they did not completely finish what they wanted to build. I suggest you also have students pause for a moment to take a deep breath and make sure they are calm and ready to share what they made. This activity can be challenging and emotional for some students to build and talk about.
7. Provide each student with the opportunity to share briefly about what they made and the emotions that it represents. Allow each student the opportunity to share at their comfort level. If a student wishes to pass, this should always be an option to ensure a safe environment. Also, let the student know, however, that if they change their mind and want to share, they can. After each student has had an opportunity to share, follow up with group discussion using the questions provided below.

Discussion Questions

1. What particular colors or emotions in your structure do you experience most often?
2. What challenges did you experience in deciding which colors to build with?
3. What is the purpose or symbolic meaning behind the structure you made?
4. In what ways does this emotion show up or affect your daily life?
5. What strategies do you use to handle these emotions?

Follow-Up or Extension Activity

- Along with the emotions color wheel, you may wish to read the story "The Color Monster" by Anna Llenas as a way to introduce students to different emotions and then have students build their own color monster using colors that represent the emotions they are experiencing. LEGO® eyes or googly eyes and tape would be helpful for this project to give the monster characters more personality.

RIPPLE EFFECTS OF CHANGE

Description of Activity

Students will build a structure that represents "ripple effects" or secondary changes that have occurred in their lives as a result of a primary change (e.g. divorce, death in the family, trauma).

Learning Objective(s)

- Students will discuss and identify secondary changes that have happened as a result of the primary change they experienced.
- Students will create and use a LEGO® structure to represent and assist them in discussing the impact of their identified secondary change.

Procedures

1. To begin this activity, explain that when major or primary change happens in our lives, we often experience a series of ripple effects or secondary changes as well that can have an impact on us. To illustrate this, ask the students if they have ever seen the ripple effect of a rock being thrown into water. You may wish to show a brief video of this and discuss how the rock impacting the water is like the change event, and the ripples that disrupt the surface are like the secondary changes that can occur as a result. An earthquake spreading from its' epicenter would also be an analogy you could use. After this, give the students an example of a real-life change situation and have the students come up with a list of ideas of potential ripple effects or secondary changes that might occur as a result of that change event. Some examples could include negative events such as getting sick, or positive events, such as being picked to be the captain of the soccer team. Discuss how sometimes the ripple effects can be positive or negative. (You may wish to use a large piece of paper or whiteboard and draw a line down the middle to have students identify and discuss potential positive changes on one side and negative changes on the other for specific change events.)

2. Next, explain that today we are going to do an activity with LEGO® bricks to help us to identify the secondary changes that have happened in our life as a result of the primary change event and explore or map how they have influenced us. To do this activity, inform students that they will be creating a structure out of LEGO® materials that represents a secondary change they have noticed that is significant to them. You may wish to encourage the students to build more than one structure if they have time leftover to represent multiple changes such as 1 positive and 1 negative. If you do not like the terms positive and negative, you could substitute the words comfortable and uncomfortable instead.

3. To help the participants better understand the activity and what types of things they might consider building, offer some ideas such as creating a LEGO® structure in the shape of an animal, person, or a certain object that they feel is representative of their emotions in some way. (An example could be if parents divorcing is the primary change,

secondary changes that are represented in a LEGO® structure could include being sad that you don't get to see one parent as often or being happy that you get to go to a new school with new friends.)

4. As students are working, confer with each member of the group regarding what they are making, the changes represented, and what they would like to share with the group about their work. This provides an opportunity to connect with each student and allows each student to rehearse what they would like to say to the whole group when it is time to share and discuss.

5. To help students transition, let them know when it is almost time to share and reassure them that it is okay if they did not completely finish what they wanted to build. I suggest you also have students pause for a moment to take a deep breath and make sure they are calm and ready to share what they made. This activity can be challenging and emotional for some students to build and talk about.

6. Provide each student with the opportunity to share briefly about what they made and the changes that it represents. Allow each student the opportunity to share at their comfort level. If a student wishes to pass, this should always be an option to ensure a safe environment. Also, let the student know, however, that if they change their mind and want to share, they can. After each student has an opportunity to share, follow up with group discussion using the questions provided below.

Discussion Questions

1. When did you first notice these secondary changes?
2. Have you experienced any unexpected secondary changes?
3. In what ways have these changes been most challenging?
4. How are these changes affecting or influencing you on a daily basis?
5. What strategies can help you to manage or cope with these changes?

Follow-Up or Extension Activity

- Using the idea of a major change event and secondary changes being like an earthquake and seismic waves, share with students sample images of earthquake maps that show the epicenter and rings that spread out from the center to show the affected area. Have the students create their own earthquake map showing their major change event as the epicenter and then have them draw additional circles that spread out across their paper. On each of the circular lines, have the students write examples of secondary changes that have occurred. You could also discuss the Richter scale and discuss with the students that the measurement of the earthquake's impact is greater as you move in toward the epicenter. Students can incorporate this idea into their earthquake map by placing secondary events of greater significance closer to epicenter. For example, if a student places "divorce" at the epicenter, they may place moving in with grandparents in the ring closest to the epicenter to designate it as a more significant or impactful secondary change. Riding the bus home from school because their mom isn't able to pick them up everyday might be farther out because they don't feel it has had as much of an impact.

ACTIVITY 1.4

INVASION OF THE ANTS

Description of Activity

Students will build bugs that represents automatic negative thoughts (ANTs) that occur as a result of the changes in their life and discuss strategies to promote positive thinking and self-talk.

Learning Objective(s)

- Students will be able to identify negative thoughts and beliefs they have as a result of life changes.
- Students will create and use a LEGO® structure to assist them in deconstructing negative self-talk and discussing strategies to support positive self-talk.

Procedures

1. Begin this activity by showing students a picture of someone who is about to do something that looks challenging. For example, it could be a photo of a person getting ready to climb a mountain, an athlete walking into a sports stadium, or a performer on stage in front of an audience. Explain to the students that when faced with a challenging situation, the way we think or our talking to ourselves (self-talk) can play a big role in our ability to be successful. Next, tell the students that we are going to work together to think of examples of positive self-talk and negative self-talk that the individual in the picture might be thinking. You may wish to use a piece of paper or whiteboard and draw a line down the middle and label one side "positive self-talk" and the other side "negative self-talk." Ask the students to come up with examples for each and make a list.
2. Next, ask the students if they have ever been in a situation where they were facing a challenge and to give examples of how positive or negative self-talk impacted them in that situation.
3. After this, show students a picture of an ant. Explain to the students, that when we have negative self-talk, this is sometimes referred to as ANTs or Automatic Negative Thoughts (Amen Clinics, 2016). You may wish to write this down so the students can see it. Explain that automatic negative thoughts can come up in lots of different situations and cause us to feel sad, angry, or even afraid. Like real ants, our automatic negative thoughts can show up in large numbers and create problems. (At this point, you might want to show the students a picture or video of ants swarming or taking over something. I like to use a cartoon image of ants marching away with delicious food from a picnic and discuss how the fruit, pie, or other food represents our positive thoughts and feelings and that we have to find ways to stop the ANTs from taking over.)
4. Next, explain to the students that after we have a difficult experience or go through a major change, sometimes ANTs like to show up and we might have a lot of negative thinking or self-talk. An example could be if someone gets a bad grade on a test, the ANTs might

show up as thoughts like "I am never going to be good at math" or "I can't do anything right." If parents announce that they are getting a divorce, the ANTs might be "This is all my fault" or "If I didn't get in trouble so much, maybe this wouldn't have happened. I'm just a bad kid." After this, explain that today they are going to make ants out of LEGO® materials and reflect on any negative thoughts or beliefs that they might have about the change event that happened in their life. To do the activity, students will create an ant or any other insect they want out of LEGO® materials. If you do an online image search for "LEGO® bugs" you should be able to find some ideas. Additionally, you may wish to provide sticky notes and something for students to write with. Instruct the students that as they are building their LEGO® structure and reflecting, they may want to write down examples of ANTs that they have had regarding the change event.

5. As students are working, confer with each member of the group regarding what they are making, examples of ANTs they have identified, and what they would like to share with the group. This provides an opportunity to connect with each student and allows each student to rehearse what they would like to say to the whole group when it is time to share and discuss.

6. To help students transition, let them know when it is almost time to share and reassure them that is okay if they did not completely finish what they wanted to build. I suggest you also have students pause for a moment to take a deep breath and make sure they are calm and ready to share what they made. This activity can be challenging and emotional for some students as negative thoughts can be associated with strong feelings such as guilt, shame, or anger.

7. Provide each student with the opportunity to share briefly about what they made and the ANTs that it represents. Allow each student the opportunity to share at their comfort level. If a student wishes to pass, this should always be an option to ensure a safe environment. Let the student know, however, that if they change their mind and want to share, they can. After each student has an opportunity to share, follow up with group discussion using the questions provided below. (You may want to have students share positive self-talk statements to confront the ANT's as they dismantle their LEGO® structure).

Discussion Questions

1. Which ANTs are the most common for you and when do they usually show up?
2. When ANTs do show up, what emotions do you experience?
3. How do ANTs affect you in your daily life or what challenges do they create?
4. What are some ways that you can be more aware of the ANTs and stop them?
5. What are some positive thoughts you would like to have instead and how can you find ways to practice the habit of using positive self-talk to challenge the ANTs?

Follow-Up or Extension Activity

- Using the analogy of a picnic, have students create a picnic basket of positive thoughts. This could be done with paper or made out of LEGO® bricks by creating different food items and writing down examples of positive thoughts to go with each food item.

FLOWERS IN BLOOM

Description of Activity

Students will build flowers that represents a lesson they have learned or a way they have grown as a result of the change.

Learning Objective(s)

- Students will discuss how change can lead to growth and identify ways the changes they have experience have helped them grow.
- Students will build and use their LEGO® structure to assist them in describing the identified lesson learned or a way they have grown personally.

Procedures

1. Begin this lesson by showing students a picture of a flower seed. Ask the students what they think the flower will need to grow (e.g. soil, sunlight, rain, air). Explain, that sometimes flowers will get rained on and go through some big storms, but still grow and bloom. Explain that in life, we may go through some very difficult storms or adversity, but often at the end of it, we find that we have learned some important lessons or we have grown as a person. (To further illustrate this concept, I often like to share an example of a famous person that they will recognize, such as an athlete, who overcame difficult circumstances to become successful.)

2. Next, explain that today we are going to do an activity with LEGO® bricks to help us to explore lessons we have learned or ways we have grown since the change event happened. Explain that sometimes it can be hard to see how we have grown, but it is important to reflect on it and learn to recognize the things we are learning and doing well. Let the students know that If they don't think there is anything, that you would like them to think of something that they would like to grow in or get better at.

3. Explain to the students that to represent the growth they have experienced, they will be building a flower or plant using LEGO® materials. Let the students know they can build any type of flower or plant they choose, and that their flower can have certain features to represent different things. For example, it could be tall or short, certain colors, or have other things "growing" on it. As an example, I could make an apple tree and talk about how each apple represents a positive or "fruitful" experience in my life that has happened. (To give students ideas on how they might choose to build their structure, you may wish to share some sample images or flowers, trees, or plants made from LEGO® materials by doing an online image search.)

4. As students are working, confer with each member of the group regarding what they are making, the growth represented, and what they would like to share with the group about their work. This provides an opportunity to connect with each student and allows each

student to rehearse what they would like to say to the whole group when it is time to share and discuss.

5. To help students transition, let them know when it is almost time to share and reassure them that is okay if they did not completely finish what they wanted to build. I suggest you also have students pause for a moment to take a deep breath and make sure they are calm and ready to share what they made. This activity can be challenging and emotional for some students to build and talk about.

6. Provide each student with the opportunity to share briefly about what they made and the growth it represents. Allow each student the opportunity to share at their comfort level. If a student wishes to pass, this should always be an option to ensure a safe environment. Also, let the student know, however, that if they change their mind and want to share, they can. After each student has an opportunity to share, follow up with group discussion using the questions provided below.

Discussion Questions

1. Does your flower or plant have any special characteristics that represent who you are or how you have grown?
2. What has been most challenging about going through this change and in what ways have you been successful in handling it?
3. What extra "sunshine" or positive factors (people, events, etc.) have helped you grow after the change event?
4. In what ways do you want to continue to grow?
5. What steps can you take or support do you need to help you to achieve the growth you want?

Follow-Up or Extension Activity

- Students will take their reflection "deeper" by exploring the roots of their plant or the personal qualities and values they possess that help them grow. To do this activity, students will place their flower or plan on top of a piece of paper and draw roots as if they were coming out of the LEGO® structure. On each root, students will write an example of a character trait or personal value that they have, such as perseverance, gratitude, determination, kindness, or courage. Students will share and discuss their character traits. Suggest that students draw some of their roots larger or smaller to show traits that are still growing or traits that more strongly define their character.

FINDING YOUR RAINBOW

Description of Activity

Students will build a rainbow or other structure that represents a positive outcome due to the change event and/or how they are moving forward.

Learning Objective(s)

- Students will be able to identify any positive outcomes that occurred after the change event.
- Students will build and use their LEGO® structure to assist them in describing the positive change and the next steps that will help them continue moving forward.

Procedures

1. Begin this lesson by showing students a picture of a rainbow. Ask the students to describe how the rainbow makes them feel or what it represents (e.g. happiness, hope, peace). Discuss with the students what happens before a rainbow appears (e.g. rain, storms). Explain that sometimes in life we will go through difficult storms and circumstances, but often at the end of it, we will find that there is a rainbow or positive outcome that will appear. Discuss with the students that over the last several weeks, they have been exploring how their life is different since the change event occurred, and that they have developed different strategies to move forward with the change.
2. Next, explain that today we are going to do an activity with LEGO® bricks to help us to explore what "rainbows" we have found in our story after the past several weeks and discuss what we hope to see in our "next chapter," or what goals we are setting for ourselves and the strategies we will use to continue to be successful in coping with the changes we have gone through.
3. Explain to the students that to explore the positive outcomes of what they have experienced, they will be building a structure with LEGO® materials to represent something that gives them hope, encouragement, or that they are looking forward to. Possible examples of things students might build could be a heart that represents the closeness and deeper appreciation they have found in their family after the loss of a loved one, or a sculpture of themselves doing an activity they enjoy that represents using the pain of the change event as motivation to be their best self and their goal to continue getting better at that activity. Students can choose anything that is personal and meaningful to them. Alternatively, if this is too open-ended and you would like to provide more structure, you may wish to have students build a rainbow and then discuss what positive outcome it represents for them.
4. As students are working, confer with each member of the group regarding what they are making, the positive outcome represented, and what they would like to share with the

group about their work. This provides an opportunity to connect with each student and allows each student to rehearse what they would like to say to the whole group when it is time to share and discuss.

5. To help students transition, let them know when it is almost time to share and reassure them that is okay if they did not completely finish what they wanted to build. I suggest you also have students pause for a moment to take a deep breath and make sure they are calm and ready to share what they made. This activity can be challenging and emotional for some students to build and talk about.

6. Provide each student with the opportunity to share briefly about what they made and the positive outcome it represents. Allow each student the opportunity to share at their comfort level. If a student wishes to pass, this should always be an option to ensure a safe environment. Also, let the student know, however, that if they change their mind and want to share, they can. After each student has an opportunity to share, follow up with group discussion using the questions provided below.

Discussion Questions

1. In what ways has seeing your "rainbow" or the positive outcomes helped you in dealing with this change event?
2. Even though you may have found some positive outcomes, what challenges are you still facing?
3. As you have participated in this group, what strategies have you developed that have been most helpful in dealing with those challenges?
4. As you move forward, there is always the chance that there will be another storm or challenge ahead. What lessons have you learned that will help you with future events?
5. Moving into your next chapter and thinking about the LEGO® structure you built today, what are you most looking forward to?

Follow-Up or Extension Activity

- Superheroes often have an origin story that describes a challenging event that leads to them acquiring their superpowers, such as being bitten by a radioactive spider. Using the change event as a catalyst, have students create their own origin story comic book of themselves that portrays them becoming a superhero and developing certain "superpowers" or character traits and strategies that they have developed as a result of the changes they have gone through. Students can create their own superhero name and costume and draw pictures of their character performing superhero feats that represent themselves overcoming their own challenges that they have faced. For example, their superhero could be shown using super strength and positive self-talk to defeat a mutant ant to represent the power of positive thinking to defeat ANTs (automatic negative thoughts).

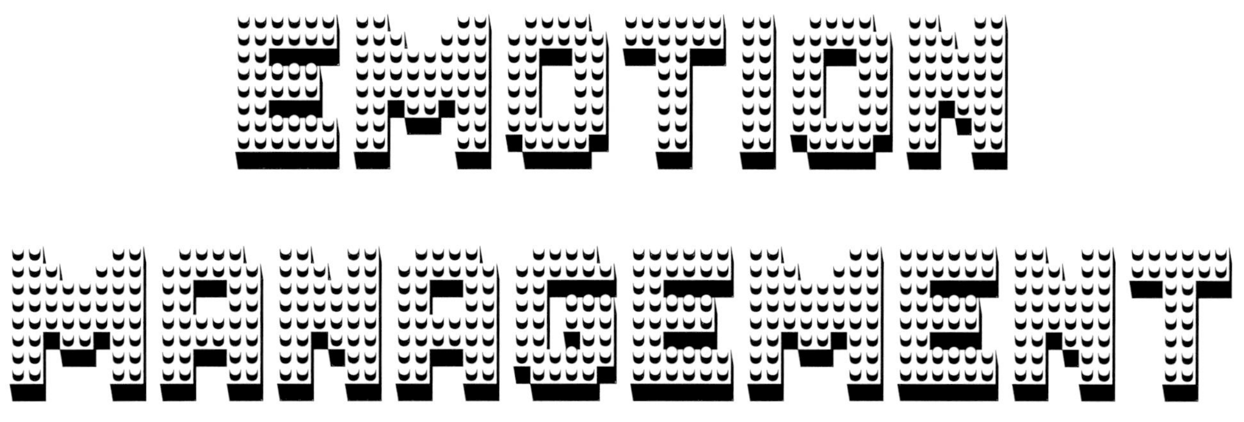

EMOTION MANAGEMENT

SECTION 2

In this section, you will find activities to support students with emotion management. Activities are designed to support students with exploring and identifying emotions, recognizing physical clues, and strategies for calming down.

RAINBOW OF EMOTIONS

Description of Activity

Students will use multiple colors representing different emotions to create a rainbow and discuss situations when they feel each of the feelings in their rainbow. In this activity, each color will represent a different emotion and students can build their rainbows using colors that correspond with the feelings they think they experience most.

Learning Objective(s)

- Students will identify emotions that they experience most often and choose a color to represent each emotion.
- Students will create a rainbow using LEGO® materials to represent and describe their most commonly experienced emotions.

Additional Materials Needed

- Paper
- Markers

Procedures

1. To begin this activity, have the students develop a list of as many emotions as they can think of in about 2 minutes. You may wish to set a timer to make it seem more like a game to get students engaged. Write down the emotions as they are shared. If possible, use a slightly large sheet of butcher paper or a whiteboard and have the students write down the emotion words.

2. Next, assign a color to each emotion by marking a different color next to each emotion word. Related emotions such as "mad" and "frustrated" may end up having the same color. If there are significant emotions missing from the list or a color is not yet used, you can suggest that the students add that color and then ask which emotions might be represented by that particular color. At this point, you may wish to facilitate a brief conversation using questions 1 and 2 from the discussion questions below.

3. After this, instruct students that they will be creating a rainbow that will include color layers that represent the emotions that they experience most frequently. Demonstrate for the students how to build a simple rainbow structure with LEGO® bricks. You may wish to do an online image search for ideas. (I would suggest asking the students to include 3-5 colors or emotions in their rainbow. On occasion, students may want to be more creative and create layer in their rainbow that includes multiple colors. I let the students know this is okay as long as they can tell me what the different colors mean or represent in terms of their emotions.) I recommend that you have colors already presorted into different containers for this activity.

4. As the students are building their rainbows, check in with each student individually to discuss which colors or emotions they are choosing and what led them to that decision. Also, remind the students to make their rainbow original by choosing colors that represent the emotions they actually experience often.

5. Once students have had a chance to complete their rainbow, have them pause and take a deep breath. For some students, this exercise can be difficult if they have some unpleasant emotions that they are reflecting on and choosing to portray in their LEGO® structure. Emotions like anger, fear, anxiety, or embarrassment can be challenging to process and talk about, so it is important for students to have a moment to breathe and find a sense of calm before moving onto the next step and having students share about their structures.

6. Now that students have had a chance to take a deep breath, explain that we will go around the table and everyone will have an opportunity to share about their rainbow. It is important to stress that this is a safe space and that what students choose to share is confidential and they can share at their own comfort level. I suggest that you have each student choose one emotion from their rainbow that they feel comfortable talking about with the group. Give students a moment to think about which one they want to share and to give a thumbs up when they are ready. Then, go ahead and let each student share.

7. To close the session, facilitate a group discussion using the remaining discussion questions below.

Discussion Questions

1. What is a strong emotion from your list that you experience often?
2. What are some situations where you could have several of these emotions at the same time?
3. Which emotion from your rainbow do you find to be most challenging to handle?
4. What strategies can you use to handle strong emotions?
5. What are some situations that are coming up this week when you think one of these emotions could happen and how can you prepare yourself to handle it successfully?

Follow-Up or Extension Activity

- If students are not excited about the idea of creating a rainbow, you could have them create alternate objects still using multiple colors to represent different emotions. Alternate things they could build in place of a rainbow could include an emotion robot, a house, a tree, or a rocket ship. It really could be anything that is of interest to the student as long the colors are chosen intentionally to represent different emotions.

MAGIC WAND

Description of Activity

Students will build a magic wand using LEGO® materials and discuss emotions and related situations they "wish" they could manage better as well as realistic strategies for effectively doing so.

Learning Objective(s)

- Students will identify situations or aspects of their life that they would like to change.
- Students will create a magic wand with LEGO® materials to help them discuss changes they would like to make.

Procedures

1. To begin this activity, it is fun to start with a brief video of a magic trick or to actually perform a simple magic trick for the students.
2. Next, talk with the students about how sometimes we can be faced with situations in life where we might wish that we had a magic wand that we could wave and magically change things. A good way to illustrate this idea is to share a story about a time where maybe you did something that was embarrassing, such as spilling something or knocking something over. Ask the students if they have any similar stories or situations that they wish they could have changed.
3. After this, instruct the students that we will be creating a magic wand out of LEGO® materials. To begin, you may wish to show the students some examples of photos of magic wands such as those featured in the Harry Potter® films to help them develop an idea for what they want their own wand to look like. Before the students start building, explain that we will be discussing situations that we wish we could change and that you would like them to reflect on something they could share with the group when they are done making their wand. This will allow the students an opportunity to process and reflect on what they want to discuss.
4. Next, have the students build their wands. Depending on how much detail students want to put into their wands, it is likely that it should only take about 3-5 minutes for students to build their wands.
5. As the students are building, begin to facilitate a group conversation using question 1 from the discussion questions below. When students are done building their wands, give each student a turn to present their wand and briefly talk about any special features their wand has.
6. After this, remind students that before they started building, you asked them to think of a situation they wish they could change. Some students may share some very personal or sensitive examples, so this is good time to review confidentiality and let students know that they can share at their comfort level. Go around the table and give each student

an opportunity to share. Pause after each student shares to do a deep breath and thank them for sharing.

7. After each student has an opportunity to share, facilitate a group discussion using the remaining discussion questions below.

Discussion Questions

1. If your magic wand could grant you three wishes, what would you wish for?
2. What are some emotions that you experience around the situation you shared?
3. How do you think things would be different if you could change the situation you shared?
4. Sometimes the situations we want to change are not in our control, but we can learn to cope with them better. What strategies or "magic tricks" (e.g. positive self-talk, deep breathing) can help you deal with those situations?
5. If your situation is something you can change, what steps are you taking or can you take to make a positive difference?

Follow-Up or Extension Activities

- An alternate version of this activity that you might like to try is to have students create a time machine. Students will create their LEGO® structure and discuss a situation they would like to go back in time to change. Students can discuss how the situation made them feel, how it has affected them, and what they would do differently if they could go back.
- To help students learn to handle strong emotions, have them create a list of "magic spells" or positive self-talk statements they can use to help them stay calm. Have students discuss which situations they might need to use these statements in to help them be successful.

ACTIVITY 2.3

BRICK BODIES

Description of Activity

Students will create a body figure out of LEGO® bricks as well as label and discuss different body responses related to different emotions.

Learning Objective(s)

- Students will be able to identify different body responses to various emotions.
- Students will create a LEGO® structure to help identify their own body responses to a particular emotion that they experience often.

Additional Materials Needed

- Paper
- Markers
- Pencils
- Scissors
- Tape

Procedures

1. Start by working with the students to create a short list of emotions that are either comfortable or uncomfortable. Next, draw 2 stick figure people and label them as comfortable and uncomfortable. Have the students come up with examples of things that happen in their body when they experience comfortable and uncomfortable emotions and write or draw them on the figures. Examples could be a fast or calm heart rate, smiling or frowning, tight or relaxed muscles, etc. (You may prefer to have examples of body responses printed off and cut out prior to the session to do this as a sorting activity.)
2. Next, give the students some examples of strong emotions and have them share what they think would happen in their bodies for each one. (Suggest about 3-4 emotions such as angry, sad, excited, or worried.)
3. After this, explain that we will be making a person out of LEGO® pieces that represents a strong feeling that they have often experienced. Then discuss the body responses that the students have when they experience that emotion. Prior to building, have the students think about a time when they had a strong emotion and how their body reacted to that emotion. Tell them not to share it yet because they are going to build their person based on that situation and then they will share their situation when they are done building.
4. Next, have the students begin building their person out of LEGO® bricks. The structure should be quite simple. (You may want to show some examples you found online). You

may also suggest that the students build their person using a color that represents the emotion they have chosen; similar to what they did in the rainbow activity from a prior session.

5. As the students are creating their person, give each student a small piece of a paper (a sticky note works great) and a pencil. When the students are done building, have the students write or draw on their paper the different body responses their person might experience based on their emotion. This activity works best if each time they write or draw something, the students cut it out with scissors and then tape it to their person. For example, if they draw an angry face, have them cut it out and put it on, then go back and write or draw their next body response. Provide extra paper as needed.
6. When students are completely done, have them pause and take a deep breath. Next, take turns letting each student share what they have created including the emotion and body responses. If they are comfortable doing so, let them also share an example of a time when they actually experienced that emotion and body responses.
7. Close the session by facilitating a discussion using the questions below.

Discussion Questions

1. Which emotions do you have most often and what are the clues in your body that let you know how you feel?
2. What kinds of emotional situations are more challenging for you to handle?
3. What are some strategies you use to stay calm?
4. What is an example of a time when you recognized you were having strong emotions and you used your calm down strategies to be successful?
5. How can you be more aware of your body signals so that you can remember to use your calm down strategies before your emotions get stronger?

Follow-Up or Extension Activities

- If you would like to further explore body responses to different emotions, you can print off blank figures and have students draw facial expressions and label different body responses. Students can compile these sheets together to make a booklet of emotions.
- An alternate version of this activity is to have students focus on a specific body response they typically experience with certain emotions and to create a LEGO® structure representing that. For example, a student with frequent stomach aches due to anxiety might create a model of a stomach out of LEGO® materials or they might be more creative and make a butterfly to represent having "butterflies in their stomach." Another example could be a student making a lighting bolt to represent stress or headaches.

CALM CREATIONS

Description of Activity

Students will create a LEGO® sculpture of an activity that is personally calming and share with the group.

Learning Objective(s)

- Students will identify activities that help them feel calm.
- Students will create a LEGO® structure to depict and discuss an activity that is personally calming.

Procedures

1. To begin this activity, I like to start by discussing the word stress. Have students define what they think the word means and provide examples of situations that could be stressful. Next, discuss examples of positive and calming activities that people might like to do if they are feeling a lot of stress. Examples might include exercise, reading, listening to relaxing music, spending time with loved ones, or doing a hobby. You may wish to share a personal example of something you enjoy doing when you are stressed.
2. Next, let the students know that we will be creating a model with LEGO® materials that represents a calming activity that they like to do. It is helpful if you have an example of something that you have created beforehand to illustrate what they could do. A person who enjoys fishing might make a LEGO® fish or a person that plays music might make a LEGO® guitar. Check to see if all students have an idea for what they want to build.
3. Once students are ready, have them begin building. As they are building, check in with each student individually and begin to facilitate a group conversation using questions 1 and 2.
4. When students are done building their LEGO® structures, provide each student with an opportunity to share what they have made.
5. Next, facilitate a discussion around the calming activities the students selected using the remaining discussion questions.
6. Close the session by having the students close their eyes and visualize that they are doing their calming activity right now. Ask them to take a deep breath and share what they are doing and how they feel.

Discussion Questions

1. On a scale of 1-10, with 1 being the lowest and 10 the highest, what would you rate your current stress level and why?
2. What types of situations can cause your stress level to go up or down?
3. How did you first discover or start the calming activity that you built today?
4. Who are some of your friends, family members, or people that you enjoy doing your selected activity with?
5. What are some of the calming activities that others shared today that you would like to try or learn more about?

Follow-Up or Extension Activity

- At the beginning of this session, you may have shared with the students an example of something you like to do that is calming. If practical to do so, you may consider providing the students an opportunity to try this activity. For example, if you like to make origami, put together puzzles, draw, write poetry, etc., these may all be activities that you could have the students try together at the end of the session. Likewise, you could let the students share their own activities or teach them to the group if practical to do so.

ACTIVITY 2.5

GRATITUDE SCULPTURES

Description of Activity

Students will create a LEGO® sculpture of something that they are grateful for in life and discuss the importance of recognizing positive things as a way to help maintain a positive outlook and work through difficult emotional situations.

Learning Objective(s)

- Students will be able to define the word gratitude and explain how it helps build a positive mindset.
- Students will identify something they are grateful for and create a LEGO® sculpture that represents that.

Additional Materials Needed

- Paper
- Markers

Procedures

1. Begin this activity by discussing the meaning of the word gratitude. As a group, create a list of things they are thankful for. Next, share with the students that focusing on gratitude can help us to maintain a positive attitude and remember to look for the good in situations even when it might be difficult. It may be helpful to share an example of a story that includes a "silver lining" or depicts how a challenging situation led to some unexpected positive outcomes. For example, in Star Wars®, Luke Skywalker crash landed in a swamp on the planet Dagobah, but then he met Yoda who trained him to use the force and helped him on his path to become a Jedi Master. You could also share a real-life example such as losing a sports game and learning from your mistakes to get better at playing the game. Explain that by focusing on what we are grateful for in a difficult situation, it can help us to overcome the challenges and strong emotions like anger, frustration, or disappointment.
2. Next, explain that we are going to create something out LEGO® materials that represents something we are grateful for. The students can choose something in general, or they may choose to build something that represents a difficult situation they faced and something they are grateful for that came out of it. You may wish to build an example prior to the session of something you are grateful for that you can share with the students. Check to see if the students have an idea for what they want to build.
3. Have the students begin working on their LEGO® structures. As the students are building, check in with each student to ensure they understand the purpose of the activity and to

discuss their idea for what they are going to build. Some students may struggle with coming up with their idea for this project and may need some support. If so, you can ask questions about what the student is thankful for or ask them to name situations where they faced or overcame a challenge and learned a lesson from their experience.

4. As the students are building, begin facilitating a group conversation using questions 1-2 from the discussion questions below.
5. Once students have finished building, have them pause and take a deep breath. Some students may have been reflecting on a very challenging or emotional situation they faced and it may be helpful to provide an opportunity for everyone to make sure they are calm before they begin sharing what they have made or discussing the situation they have chosen with the group.
6. When everyone is ready, give each student an opportunity to share their gratitude sculptures and discuss why they chose to make that.
7. Close the session by facilitating a discussion using the remaining discussion questions below.

Discussion Questions

1. Earlier I mentioned the story about Star Wars®. What are some other stories where the character faced a difficult situation but something good ended up coming out of it?
2. Is it easier to find things to be grateful for in the moment while something is happening or after it has already happened?
3. How can you develop an attitude of gratitude when you are in the middle of something difficult or having strong emotions?
4. What are some ways that you can start to practice gratitude more often?
5. How does the habit of gratitude help you keep your emotions calm?

Follow-Up or Extension Activities

- Students will create a LEGO® gratitude sculpture in honor of someone that they want to say thank you to. Take a picture of the LEGO® sculpture and print it to include in a thank you note that the student can give to the person they want to thank. This can be done as a community service project as well such as by having students create a fire truck and writing a thank you note to the local fire department.
- Students can begin keeping a gratitude journal and you can make gratitude sharing a regular habit by opening each session with letting each person share one thing they are thankful for that day.

ACTIVITY 2.6

POSITIVE SELF-TALK TOWERS

Description of Activity

Students will create a LEGO® tower or "skyscraper" and attach a positive self-talk statement to each brick as they are building in response to demonstrate which statements they would use in different scenarios.

Learning Objective(s)

- Students will identify different examples of positive self-talk.
- Students will demonstrate positive self-talk statements they would use in response to various scenarios.

Additional Materials Needed

- Paper
- Markers
- Pencils
- Tape

Procedures

1. Begin this activity by discussing activities that the students like to do. Make a list of these activities on a large piece of paper or whiteboard. Next, have each student share an example of a challenge that you might experience when doing these activities. For example, a student who said soccer might talk about missing a shot to make a goal. Write down one example for each activity. After this, discuss with the students which emotions they might also experience with each of the challenges, such as frustration, anger, or worry.
2. Next, discuss the difference between positive and negative self-talk. Go back to the list of activities and have students come up with an example of both positive and negative self-talk for each of the challenges identified. Discuss which type of self-talk is most likely to help them overcome or work through the challenge to be successful.
3. Then, explain to the students that we are going to be practicing using positive self-talk today and will be doing a LEGO® activity called positive self-talk towers. To begin the activity, give each student a small piece of paper (sticky tabs would be ideal for this activity, but a sticky note and tape will work fine) and a pencil. Ask the students to write down several examples of positive self-talk statements. It is okay to discuss this as a group and have students write down the same examples if they want. Each student should have their own set of about 5-10 positive self-talk statements. Next, have the students attach or tape their statements to individual LEGO® bricks.

4. After students have their self-talk bricks made, you are ready to begin the activity. Start by explaining to the students that you are going to read them examples of challenging situations and then they will choose one of their self-talk statements that they would use if they were in that situation. Read a scenario below and have the students place their chosen self-talk brick in front of them. Each time a student uses one of their self-talk bricks, it has to stay on the table and they will add a new one to their stack by connecting the bricks together to make a tower. After each scenario, give each student a chance to read their self-talk statement. As a group, you can have the students discuss which self-talk statement they like the best. If a student wants to reuse one of the statements they already used, they can rearrange their stack so that statement is on the top of the stack.

   Scenarios:

   - *You are playing basketball and have a chance to make the game-winning score.*
   - *You are learning to play a new song on the piano and it is really difficult.*
   - *You are really mad at a friend over a game at recess.*
   - *You are about to perform in the talent show.*
   - *You just found out that an event you were looking forward to has been cancelled.*

5. After you have gone through each of the scenarios, have the students reflect on which positive self-talk statement they like the most or use most frequently. Facilitate a conversation using the discussion questions listed below.

Discussion Questions

1. Which positive self-talk statement do you like the most?
2. Do you use more positive or negative self-talk and in what types of situations?
3. What is an example of a time when self-talk either helped or hindered you from being successful?
4. What situations do you want to practice using positive self-talk in more often?
5. How does self-talk affect your emotions and how can we use it to help ourselves calm strong emotions and be more successful?

Follow-Up or Extension Activity

- If students have a particular self-talk statement that they have identified as one they like, provide the students an opportunity to create a poster of that self-talk statement that they can take home and display as a reminder.

MINDFULNESS

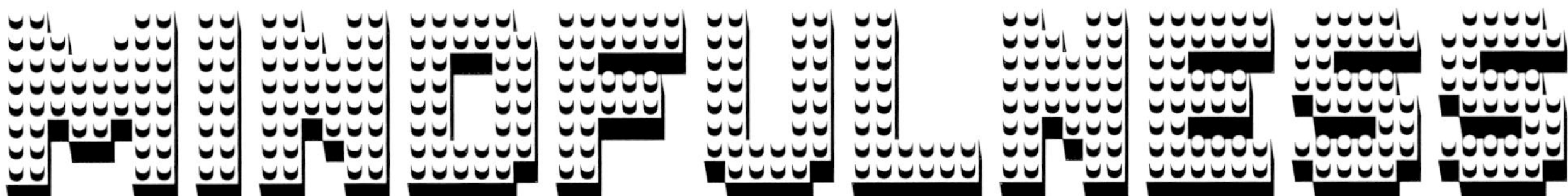

SECTION 3

In this section, you will find activities to support students with mindfulness and relaxation activities to help reduce stress and practice strategies for calmness.

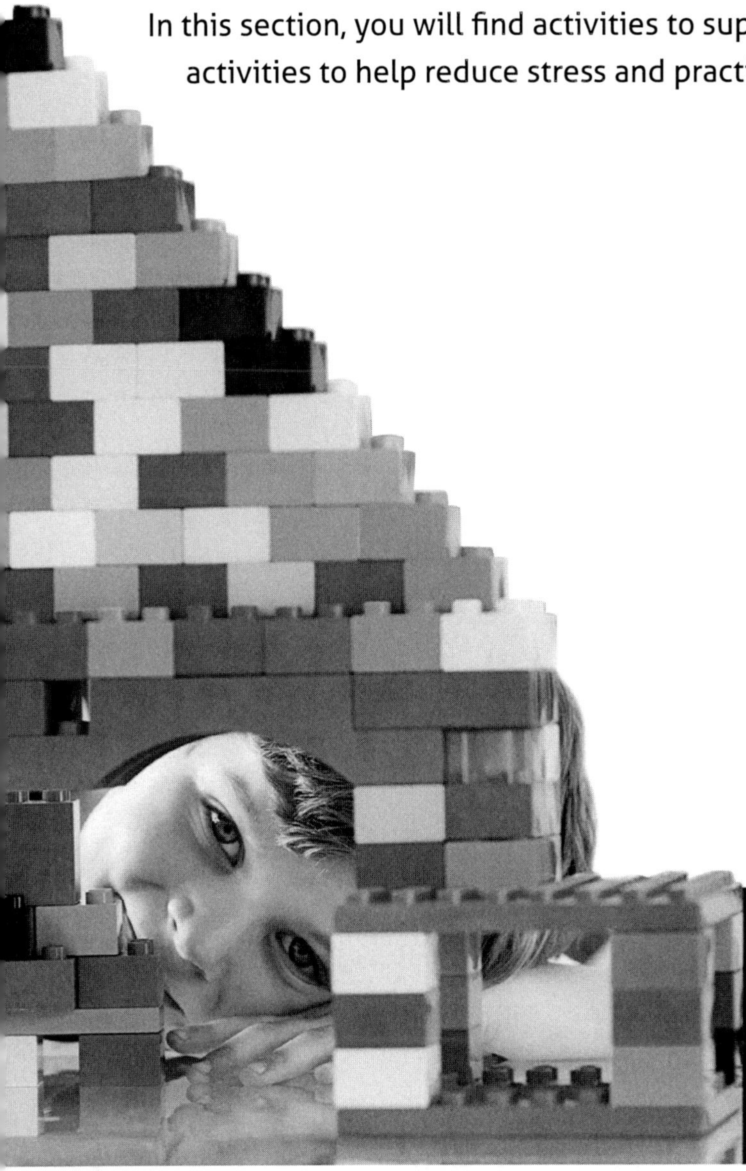

ACTIVITY 3.1

BUILDING IN HARMONY

Description of Activity

Students will build with LEGO® materials as they listen to slow, relaxing music. As the students build, they will attempt to build in harmony with the music.

Learning Objective(s)

- Students will slow their breathing and movement to synchronize with the music as they build freely with LEGO® materials.
- Students will identify how they felt while building in harmony with the music.

Additional Materials Needed

- Instrumental Music (Relaxation, Jazz, etc.)

Procedures

1. Start by asking the students if anyone can explain what the word "harmony" means. Provide a couple of examples such as dancing in sync with music or mirroring another person's body movements.
2. Next, explain that today we will be listening to some relaxing music and attempting to build a structure with LEGO® materials in harmony with the music. This could include slowing movement and breathing as they are building, building with colors or in patterns that students feel reflect the mood of the music, and even closing their eyes as they build. The structure can be representative of something that is inspired by the music or it can be completely abstract.
3. To help students better understand what they are being asked to do, let the students know that you are going to start by modeling the activity, and then ask them to join in when they are ready.
4. Turn on the music you have selected and begin modeling for the students how to build in harmony. As you are modeling, point out to the students how you are slowing your movement or even "dancing" with the LEGO® pieces as you build, controlling your breathing, or selecting certain colors based on the mood inspired by the music. Ask the students to join in when they are ready.
5. In order to support students with transition as the music finishes, let students know when the song is almost finished and that we will pause at that time.
6. At the pause, ask students to take a deep breath and take a moment to reflect on what they built and how they felt building it.

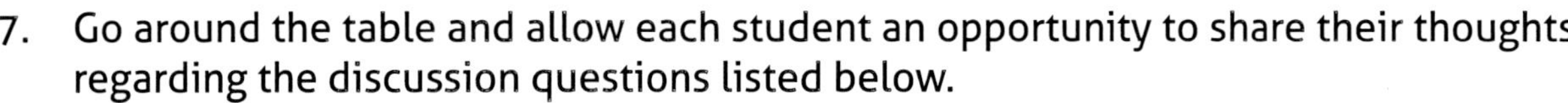

7. Go around the table and allow each student an opportunity to share their thoughts regarding the discussion questions listed below.

Discussion Questions

1. Does your structure represent anything? If so, What?
2. How did you feel as you were building your structure?
3. Take a moment to look at the structures that other group members created. What compliments you would like to share?
4. At which times during the day do you notice your body responses (breathing, movement, tension, etc.) changing most often?
5. When you notice that you are having uncomfortable body responses, what are some things you can do to help yourself feel calmer?

Follow-Up or Extension Activities

- Attempt to build a structure with a partner while breathing and moving in unison with the rhythm of the music. This can be done with each partner holding opposite ends of the same LEGO® bricks, or each person adding bricks to the structure individually. This is a great way to encourage positive connections between group members and teach body awareness and self-control as students mirror one another's movement and breathing.
- Change the style or tempo of the music to create a different experience. For example, you may wish to spend a few minutes of your session doing the activity with a very slow relaxing song, such as spa music, and then start over with a something faster or more upbeat, such as instrumental cardio workout music to elicit different responses. Then discuss with the students how they felt while doing the activity with the 2 different types of music. This is a great way to help students develop great self-awareness of their body responses. You may wish to end the session with another calm and relaxing song to help students regulate their emotions prior to transitioning back to class or the next activity.

PEACEFUL PATTERNS

Description of Activity

Students will create symmetrical patterns using LEGO® materials.

Learning Objective(s)

- Students will explore the concepts of balance and symmetry through LEGO® patterns.
- Students will identify strategies for maintaining social-emotional balance.

Additional Materials Needed

- 1 square baseplate for each student or 1 sheet of construction paper

Procedures

1. Before beginning this activity, it is important to ensure that all students have an understanding of the words symmetry and balance. I have found that an effective way to illustrate these concepts is to share photos of nature that show these characteristics such as flowers, snowflakes, or a clear mountain lake with the mountain reflecting in the water. You may also decide to share photos of mandalas or other artistic patterns. (see example in Follow-Up or Extension Activities)
2. Next, explain that today we will be creating artwork using LEGO® materials that is balanced and symmetrical. This activity works best if each student has their own individual baseplate to build on, however it can be done on a tabletop or even on a piece of construction paper.
3. Demonstrate for the students how you will go about creating a symmetrical pattern by beginning with a LEGO® brick in the center. If you are using a baseplate, find the center and place your first LEGO® brick. Explain to the students that by starting at the center, we can work our way outward and around it to ensure that we build our pattern with balance and symmetry.
4. When students place their first brick in the center, have them pause, take a deep breath, and visualize what they think their pattern might look like including the colors they want to use and what types of LEGO® pieces they want to include.
5. As students begin to build, you may wish to turn on some relaxing background music. Similar to the previous session, students could be encouraged to build in harmony with the music as they create their patterns or mandalas.
6. As the students are building, facilitate a conversation using the discussion questions.

7. At the close of the session, take a moment for everyone to share what they have made and explain what it represents.

Discussion Questions

1. How did you feel as you were building your patterns?
2. What makes you feel balanced or when do you feel most balanced?
3. What strategies can you use if you are not feeling very balanced or you have stress?
4. What is a situation where you want to work on having greater balance?
5. How does having greater balance help us overall?

Follow-Up or Extension Activities

- Separate out different colored LEGO® bricks into individual containers, resealable bags, or piles on the table. Create a list designating different emotions represented by each of the colors chosen. Share this information with the students and ask them to build their patterns as described above, but to use colors that most closely match with how they are feeling today. Emphasize that it is okay to build with more than one color as it is often possible that we will have multiple feelings that we are experiencing.
- In this activity, students are asked to begin their patterns by locating the center of their baseplate or by simply starting with a center piece. The concept of finding your center can be explored metaphorically on a deeper level and connected to deep breathing from our center to maintain a sense of calm, or establishing other strategies to stay "centered" or balanced such as positive self-talk, gratitude, or other calming activities.

Example of a Mandala

"Legomandala" combines the Tibetan Buddhist tradition of creating and ritualistically dismantling ornate sand mandalas with the contemporary medium of LEGO® bricks.

DESIGNS IN NATURE

Description of Activity

Students will create LEGO® structures that represent shapes or patters in nature. This activity can be completed indoors or outdoors.

Learning Objective(s)

- Students can select an object in nature that is appealing to them.
- Students are able to be mindful of different characteristics of their object and incorporate those features into a LEGO® model of their object.

Additional Materials Needed

- Items found in nature such as leaves, rocks, sticks, or pinecones

Procedures

1. Begin this activity by presenting various objects collected from nature prior to the group session. These objects should represent a variety of shapes, sizes, textures, colors, or other features. If it is possible, you may consider taking the students outside and providing them with an opportunity to find an object that they would like to use for this activity. Additionally, if you do not have access to actual objects from nature, this activity could also be done with photos that are printed out and presented to the students to choose from. Photos also make it possible to include choices like mountains, rivers, trees, or other items from nature.
2. Have each student select an object that appeals to them. Then ask them to hold their object, close their eyes, and take a deep breath. As the students are doing this, ask them to reflect on the different qualities of their object such as the weight, texture, color, smell, or any other characteristics they notice. If they are using a photo of an object, have students visualize the object and what characteristics it would have.
3. Give each student an opportunity to share with the group what they noticed about their object.
4. Next, explain to the students that we will be building a LEGO® model of the object they selected. Encourage the students to incorporate as much detail as they can into their design. In order to add the greatest amount of details it is best to ask the students to build their model as if it were the actual object and not as a 2-dimensional representation of it.
5. As the students are building. Remind them to reflect on the different characteristics of their object that they identified and to really try to design their LEGO® model to match those features. To do this, students can choose specific LEGO® pieces that they think will best represent that. You may also ask the students about what types of features they are

attempting to create and then provide assistance with locating bricks that would be suited for their needs. It may also help to provide scaffolding by offering the student design suggestions that match the student's identified characteristics.

6. While the students are building, periodically have the students draw comparisons between their actual object and their LEGO® model by identifying specific characteristics that are present in both. For example, a student building a pinecone may notice that the texture is prickly and they may try to incorporate this texture into their LEGO® model by having wedge bricks that protrude and mimic that texture.

7. As students are building, you may also facilitate conversation around how they feel in the moment as they are creating their nature objects. This activity can be quite challenging and sometimes frustrating for students. Completing this activity requires students to be mindful of the features of their nature objects, but there is also an opportunity for students to be mindful of their own emotions and body responses while they are building. During this time, use the questions below to help students identify and discuss the feelings they are experiencing in the moment.

8. Wrap up the session by giving each student an opportunity to share their object that they have created using the LEGO® materials. Ask the following questions to help facilitate discussion.

Discussion Questions

1. What are your feelings right now as you build your LEGO® model?
2. What sensations do you notice in your body that may be related to how you feel?
3. What challenges did you have with building your nature object with LEGO® bricks?
4. What are some strategies to keep yourself calm as you attempt this activity?
5. What are some situations when you think it would be helpful to be mindful of your feelings and body responses, and to remember to use your calm-down strategies?

Follow-Up or Extension Activity

- If you have LEGO® eyes or googly craft eyes, have the students add them to their nature object that they have made using LEGO® materials to create a character. Discuss the physical characteristics of the object and what personality traits their character might have. For example, a tree might be very strong and dependable, a bright green leaf might be very calm and positive, or a prickly pinecone might have difficulty getting along with others. Students can discuss why they chose those particular character qualities and connect them to examples of how they might show those qualities at times in their own life.

MINDFUL MIRROR

Description of Activity

Students will practice synchronized breathing, movement, and LEGO® building with a partner.

Learning Objective(s)

- Students learn to control their own breathing and movement to mirror a partner.
- Students can use effective communication skills to work together with others.

Procedures

1. Begin this activity by discussing the word synchronized with the students and sharing some examples of synchronized activities such as swimming, dancing, or even miming. You may find it helpful to share a brief video of one of these activities to help illustrate the concept of synchrony.
2. Next, explain to the group that we are going to practice being synchronized with a partner through a game called "Mindful Mirror." This game can be played with both students sitting or standing facing one another. In this game students will work with a partner to match their movement and breathing so that it is synchronized as if you are watching yourself in a mirror. Have one student start as the leader and the other student will play the role of the mirror. In this game, the student who is the mirror will need to pay close attention to the leader's actions so that they can follow along and stay synchronized. Have the leader begin the game with simple hand and arm movements and then gradually add more elements such as facial expressions or specific breathing strategies that their partner will need to copy. As the students are doing the activity, prompt them to move and breathe slowly so that their partner can keep up with the movement. As students get more proficient, you can also prompt them to try to increase their speed gradually or to make the movements more complex such as a figure 8 or tracing other shapes.
3. Once students have developed a rhythm and are able to do the activity successfully (usually about 2 minutes), have them switch roles so the other person can have a turn being the mirror or the leader.
4. After the students have both had a turn doing each role, have them pause. Before moving on to the next phase of the activity, you may wish to discuss questions 1 and 2 from the discussion questions.
5. When students are ready, introduce the next part of the activity by letting them know that we are not going to do the same thing, but this time we will be adding LEGO® bricks and building in synchrony. This activity works best if students are sitting on opposite sides of a table facing one another. Prior to beginning this activity, it is best if you have a pile of LEGO® bricks of a single color spread out on the table for the students to use.

To do the activity, the student who is playing the role of the leader will slowly begin to build using the available LEGO® materials. The student who is the mirror will have to pay close attention to the size of the brick chosen by the leader, as their goal will be to create an exact replica of what the leader is making. Having the LEGO® pieces spread out on the table makes it a little easier to find the exact same piece rather than digging in a tub.

6. As the students are attempting this activity, remind the student playing the role of the leader to move slowly at first to allow their partner to keep up. As students become more proficient, they can begin to increase their speed.
7. Before the end of the session, take a moment to discuss the remaining discussion questions below.

Discussion Questions

1. What challenges did you face in maintaining synchrony with your partner?
2. What strategies did you use to help yourselves be successful?
3. How did the level of difficulty increase when you included LEGO® bricks?
4. How did you maintain your focus while doing the activity?
5. What activities would these focus strategies help you be more successful with?

Follow-Up or Extension Activities

- If you find that it is simply too difficult for the student playing the role of the mirror to find the right pieces and build a matching structure, try having the student playing the mirror follow along with the leader's movement and actually pick up the exact same piece together. To do this successfully, the student who is the mirror must be gentle in touching the LEGO® pieces and allow the leader to be the one who directs the movement and building of the LEGO® structure. This requires self-control and can be challenging for some students. Provide prompting such as "remember to follow the leader and let them guide the movement or building." Pause and switch roles when the students are ready.
- The student can do a similar activity individually or in tandem with a partner by looking in an actual mirror. In this activity, students will build a LEGO® structure, but they will be challenged to do it by only looking at their movement in the mirror and not directly at the LEGO® pieces in front of them. This activity requires students to focus in a different way and be mindful of visual and spatial awareness.

ACTIVITY 3.5

BALANCING ACT

Description of Activity

Students will perform a series of movements and deep breathing while attempting to balance LEGO® pieces in various ways.

Learning Objective(s)

- Students will use body and spatial awareness to maintain balance of LEGO® pieces while performing different movements and deep breathing.
- Students will use effective communication skills to give and follow directions from a partner.

Procedures

1. To begin this activity, I like to start by sharing a fun video or photo of someone balancing a lot of objects, such as a circus performer or even an animal balancing a ball on their nose. Have a brief discussion with the students about the meaning of the word balance. You can also have the students provide some examples of activities where it is important to have good balance.
2. Next, tell the students that we are going to practice doing some exercises that will require them to have good balance. Start by showing the students a fun example of the type of activities you will be doing by balancing a short stack of LEGO® bricks on your nose, chin, or forehead perhaps. This may be very exciting and funny for some students, so you might want to follow up with a deep breathing exercise to help them get calm again before moving on to the next step.
3. Next, explain to the students that we are going to start out by working together and then with a partner. To begin, have the students sitting at the table and give each of them a single LEGO® brick of any size you choose. Ask them to stretch out their arm with their hand flat on the table and have them place the brick on the back side of their hand. Have the students keep it balanced for a few seconds and instruct them to take a deep breath while keeping their LEGO® piece still. Next, begin to guide the students through a series of movements while the students attempt to keep their LEGO® piece balanced. Start by asking the students to slowly raise their arms off the table to about shoulder height. Then, ask the students to move their arm side to side, up and down, or to try tracing shapes such as a figure 8, or a triangle. As the students do the movement, you may wish to incorporate some deep breathing in harmony with the arm movements. For example, if students are moving their arm up and down as they balance the LEGO® piece, you could ask them to take a deep breath in as their arm slowly moves up and then to exhale as they slowly bring their arm back down.

As students are doing this, have them track the LEGO® piece with their eyes to maintain focus on balancing it the entire time and not letting it fall off. If the piece gets dropped, simply have the students put it back on their hand and continue.

4. Once students have shown some proficiency with this, pause and discuss the experience so far using questions 1 and 2 from the discussion questions below.
5. Next, increase the difficulty by adding a LEGO® brick to the students' other hand and having them try the same movements as they balance LEGO® pieces on both hands. Have students do this for about a minute.
6. Next, let the students know that they are going to work with a partner for the next part. Assign or have students choose their partner. If there is an odd number or if you are working with an individual student, you can join in as well. Start by having the students take their 2 LEGO® bricks each and combine them with their partner's bricks to make a stack of 4. For the next part, have students stand and hold the stack of bricks together. They can hold it any way they want as long as both of them are touching it, however, to make it more challenging, you can ask the students to balance the bricks as a team using only one finger. Next, instruct them through a series of movements such as to raise and lower the LEGO® bricks, move them in a circular motion, a zig-zag, or to trace a simple shape like a square, or a more complex shape like a star. As students are doing these movements, remind students to breathe in and out with their movements and provide prompting such as "go at the right pace so your partner can follow along" or "remember to keep your eyes on the LEGO® piece so you can track it and keep it balanced".
7. If you still have time, let the students take on the role of being a leader by giving verbal directions. This is similar to the "Mindful Mirror" game, but this time one student will say what movements they want to do and their partner will initiate the movement.
8. To close the session, discuss the remaining discussion questions below.

Discussion Questions

1. On a scale of 1-10 with 1 being super easy and 10 being super hard, how difficult was it to keep up with the movements and balancing your LEGO® piece?
2. What strategies or techniques did you use to help keep the LEGO® piece balanced?
3. When working with a partner, what was different or more challenging?
4. What activities or things in your life are difficult for you to balance?
5. What strategies help you keep those things balanced in life?
6. Like your partner in this activity, who is someone that helps you stay balanced?

Follow-Up or Extension Activity

- If the activity is too easy for some students, add to the level of difficulty by having them balance a LEGO® piece on their forehead or by adding a second or larger stack of bricks. You can also have them balance on one foot or try other positions.

ACTIVITY 3.6

GARDENS OF THE MIND

Description of Activity

Students will design a small garden using LEGO® materials.

Learning Objective(s)

- Students will identify elements of gardens that provide a sense of calm.
- Students will create their own design for a garden using LEGO® materials.

Additional Materials Needed

- Baseplates or construction paper

Procedures

1. To begin this activity, share photos or a brief video of a various styles of gardens. Discuss the various features that students notice and what they like about different types of gardens. Features might include pathways, a pond, rock features, bridges, or certain types of plants. One of the most important concepts to emphasize is that gardens are often designed to be a calm and peaceful space and that one of our goals today is to try to incorporate that into our design for our garden.
2. Next explain to the students that we are going to have the opportunity to make our own garden using LEGO® materials. This activity can be done individually or with a partner. Before starting, give each student an opportunity to share what elements they think they would like to include in their garden. You may find it helpful for some students if you provide them with a piece of blank paper and a pencil and have them draw a picture of what they would like their garden to look like before they share their ideas and start building. (You may want to show the photo of plants made with LEGO® bricks at the end of Follow-Up or Extension Activity).
3. Once students have had a chance to share, pass out baseplates of construction paper for the students to build their gardens on and have them begin working. As the students are working, you may want to turn on some relaxing background music.
4. While the students are working, check with each student about how their project is progressing and what elements they are including in their gardens.
5. After you have checked in with each student, facilitate a group discussion using the discussion questions.
6. After students have finished building, give each student an opportunity to share their garden and a couple of their favorite features included in their design.

7. Finish the session by having each student close their eyes and visualize that they are sitting or taking a stroll inside their garden. Ask the students to take a deep breath and then go around the table and have each student share one thing they can see, smell, hear, or notice as they are visiting their garden.

Discussion Questions

1. Have you ever visited a garden before and what was it like?
2. What are some natural features, flowers, or other things that you appreciate that you tried to include in your garden design?
3. If you were a flower or another feature in your garden, what would you be and why?
4. Gardens are often a place where people go to relax. What is your favorite place to go to relax or somewhere you have been that was very peaceful?
5. What other activities do you like to do to help you feel calm or reduce stress?

Follow-Up or Extension Activity

- If you have access to craft materials such as artificial flowers or moss, or actual small nature items such as rocks or twigs, students may enjoy incorporating these items into their gardens. While this can make for a more engaging and interesting experience for the students, it will also require more work to clean up, so you may want to limit how much extra material you provide.

Carnivorous plants made with LEGO® bricks at Gardens By The Bay in Singapore

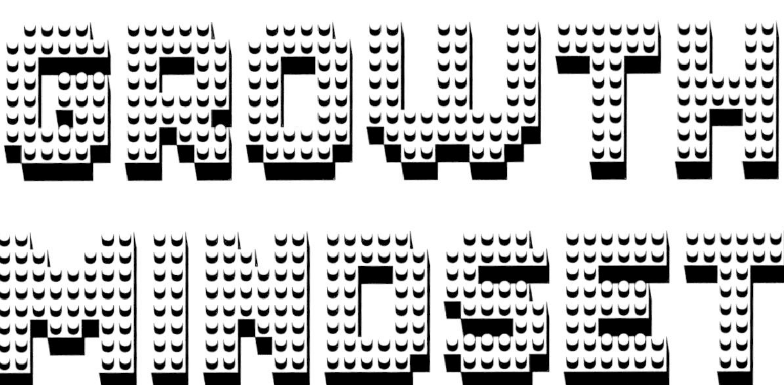

GROWTH MINDSET

SECTION 4

In this section, you will find activities to support students with growth mindset and resilience by exploring various topics such as goal setting, positive thinking, overcoming failure, and strategies for success.

ACTIVITY 4.1

RISING AGAINST THE ODDS

Description of Activity

Students will discuss perseverance and build a LEGO® structure that represents a time when they had to overcome a difficulty or challenge in life.

Learning Objective(s)

- Students will discuss emotions associated with experiencing failure and setbacks.
- Students will build a structure representing a time when they showed perseverance toward a goal.

Additional Materials Needed

- Game Dice

Procedures

1. Begin this session by discussing the word perseverance. Ask the students if they can provide a definition or examples of what the word means. You may wish to write down their ideas on a piece of paper or whiteboard. Next, you may wish to share a brief story or video of a "famous failure" or a well-known person who failed many times in life but eventually found success through perseverance.

2. Next, let the students know we are going to do a short game to illustrate perseverance. To play this game, you will need a pair of dice. Students will begin to build a tower using LEGO® materials, but every 30 seconds, they will pause and someone will roll the dice. Whatever number comes up on the dice is the number of LEGO® bricks that students will need to remove from their structure (e.g. if they roll a 9, they will remove 9 bricks from their tower). Then they will start to build again and after another 30 seconds, you will roll the dice again and have them remove the matching number of pieces. For younger students, you may wish to only use one die. You may also want to give your students a goal for how many bricks they are trying to include in their tower (e.g. 30 bricks). Students will discuss the emotions experienced as they had to take apart what they had built and their strategies to overcome the challenge.

3. After this, facilitate a conversation using questions 1-2 from the discussion questions.

4. Next, explain that you want everyone to think of a time when they showed perseverance toward a goal. It could be something that they were successful at overcoming or it can be something where they did not reach their goal. It could also be something they are persevering toward currently. Let the students know that they will be building something out of LEGO® materials to represent their goal that they want to share with the group. When everyone has an idea for what they want to make, have the students begin building their LEGO® structures.

5. As they are building, check in with each student to discuss what they have chosen to make and how it demonstrates or relates to perseverance.
6. When they are finished building, have each student present what they made and explain how their LEGO® structure represents a time when they demonstrated perseverance.
7. Close the session by facilitating a conversation with the remaining discussion questions.

Discussion Questions

1. In our LEGO® game, every time you made progress, you rolled the dice and you had to go backwards. Have you ever felt this way about a goal in real life?
2. When you are faced with a challenge, what emotions or thoughts do you usually experience?
3. Who is someone you know or look up to that you think shows a lot of perseverance?
4. In what ways is perseverance something that you can develop in yourself?
5. What strategies do you think will most help you develop your own perseverance?

Follow-Up or Extension Activity

- As a group, have the students all write down a goal that they are persevering toward on a single piece of paper. Bring this paper out at the beginning or end of each group session and do a quick check in to see how everyone is working on their goals and to offer encouragement to one another.

BUILDING ON OUR FAILURES

Description of Activity

Students will build a LEGO® structure representing a time when they experienced failure and what they learned or how they have grown as a result of that experience.

Learning Objective(s)

- Students will discuss the consequences and benefits of failure.
- Students will create a LEGO® structure representing a time when they experienced failure and discuss what they learned as a result of that experience.

Procedures

1. Begin this activity by discussing the word failure. Ask the students if they see it as good or bad and why. Usually they will see failure as a negative, so you may need to follow up by asking them to think of examples of when failure could actually be a positive thing. As in the previous session, you may find it helpful to share another story or video of a famous person who failed and discuss how they learned from their experience to get better and eventually become successful.
2. Next, have the students reflect on a time when they failed, made a mistake, or did not reach their goal. Let the students know that they will be creating 2 LEGO® structures today. The first structure will represent the failure that they experienced, and the second structure will represent what they learned or how they have grown as a result of that experience. If you do not have enough time to build 2 separate structures, have the students build the first one and then they can talk about their growth during group discussion. (You may wish to have an example for the students to develop a better concept of how to approach this activity.) If your failure event is failing a math test, you could build a number out of LEGO® materials to represent the math test, and a question mark to show that you started asking for help in class more to make sure you understood how to do the math problems correctly. When they students are ready, have them begin building their structures.
3. As the students are building, check in with each student regarding their structures and offer support as needed. Some students will need help choosing something to build that represents what they learned from their experience. If you find this is too abstract or difficult for your students, have them focus on just building a structure that represents a time when they failed at something.
4. While the students are building, you can begin a group discussion with questions 1-2 from the discussion questions.
5. When students are finished building, have them pause and take a deep breath to make sure everyone is calm and ready to discuss what they made. Reflecting on a past failure

can be an emotional task and students may need some space to self-regulate before having a conversation. When they are ready, have each student share what failure their LEGO® structure represents, what they were thinking or feeling at the time, how they handled the situation, and what they learned from the experience.

6. Close the session by discussing the remaining discussion questions below.

Discussion Questions

1. When we experience failure, sometimes we have negative self-talk. What are some examples of negative thoughts or self-talk that you find yourself repeating when you make a mistake or fail at something?
2. When you think negatively, how does it affect how you feel?
3. How can you change your thinking about failure and start to see it as an opportunity to learn and grow? What would you build to represent what you've learned?
4. If you start to change your thinking about the failure to be more positive, how will that affect your feelings in a positive way also?
5. In the experience you shared, we also talked about how we learned something as a result of that. What is a time when you had to face a similar challenge and found that you performed better or approached a problem differently due to a previous experience?

Follow-Up or Extension Activity

- After students have discussed what they have learned from their experience, have them create a growth mindset journal where they can keep track of times when they made a mistake and what they learned from that experience. When faced with a current challenge or failure, students can look back at their past experiences to remind themselves that they have faced similar situations in the past and were able to learn and grow as a result.

OBSTACLE COURSE CHALLENGE

Description of Activity

Students will build a LEGO® structure that represents a challenge they are currently facing and discuss specific obstacles that they would like to overcome, as well as positive self-talk strategies to do so.

Learning Objective(s)

- Students will identify examples of obstacles that can impede reaching their goals.
- Students will create a LEGO® structure representing a current obstacle and discuss positive self-talk strategies for overcoming that obstacle.

Procedures

1. Begin this activity by discussing the word obstacle. Ask the students to explain what an obstacle is and to give examples. Many students will think of an obstacle course when they hear this word. (To help illustrate the meaning of an obstacle I like to show the students a video clip from American Ninja Warrior® or Wipeout® where the contestants have to overcome an obstacle to get to the next stage of the course.) If you have a personal story you can share with the students that is slightly embarrassing or funny, they might enjoy hearing about your experience also! Ask the students to share if they have ever had a time when they faced a similar failure or made a mistake in front of other people and how it made them feel.

2. Next, let the students know that today we are going to be working on finding ways to overcome obstacles to achieve our goals. Explain that one of our most important strategies for success begins with our mindset. At this point, I like to share the quote "he who thinks he can, and he who thinks he can't, are both right." Ask the students to explain what they think the quote means. You may wish to also have a couple students share about a time when they either told themselves they could or could not do something and how it affected the outcome of reaching their goal.

3. After this, have the students think about a goal they are working on currently or that they had in the past. Ask them to also think about any obstacles that were present as they tried to reach that goal or that they are currently facing. Next, let the students know that they are going to make their own obstacle course using LEGO® materials. The course is going to represent their journey toward reaching a goal. They will need to include at least one obstacle that represents a challenge that they faced or are currently facing in reaching the goal. Before students start building, brainstorm some ideas as a group for what kind of obstacles they could build with LEGO® materials (e.g. climbing a wall, bridge, ring of fire, etc.).

4. When students are ready, have them begin building their obstacle course. As the students are building, check in with each student to discuss what they are making and provide support as needed. Some students may need some help constructing their obstacle courses. As the students are building, you may wish to begin facilitating a conversation using questions 1-2 from the discussion questions below.
5. After the students have finished building their obstacle course, have each student present their obstacle course and discuss what goal it represents and what the obstacles are to reaching that goal.
6. Close the session by facilitating a discussion using the remaining discussion questions below. You may also wish to finish the session by having the students close their eyes and envision that they are actually inside their obstacle course that they created. Have them imagine themselves going through the course and overcoming the obstacles to reach the goal. Ask them how it felt to reach the goal and encourage them to keep working toward their goal in real life.

Discussion Questions

1. What is the biggest physical obstacle that you have ever had to overcome? (e.g. Hiking to the top of a mountain, running a race, etc.)
2. When you were facing that challenge, what strategies did you use to be successful?
3. In your obstacle course, what strategies can you use to overcome the obstacle?
4. What is your plan to overcome obstacles in real life to achieve your current goals?
5. How can you maintain a positive mindset to help you overcome mistakes, setbacks, or fear of failure?

Follow-Up or Extension Activity

- After students have identified their goal and a current obstacle they are trying to overcome, have them draw a self-portrait of themselves passing or overcoming the obstacle to reach their goal. Have the students write an example of positive self-talk that is going through their mind as they work to overcome the obstacle. An example could be a self-portrait showing a student climbing over a wall of books to represent studying for an upcoming test, or a student singing over a pit of music notes and piano key alligators to represent learning to play a new song for an upcoming piano recital.

ACTIVITY 4.4

PHOENIX RISING

Description of Activity

Students will learn about the mythology of the phoenix and build a LEGO® structure representing a difficult situation, setback, or failure they experienced and discuss any positive outcomes that resulted from that situation.

Learning Objective(s)

- Students will discuss the mythology of the phoenix and how negative situations or failure can sometimes lead to positive outcomes.
- Students will create one LEGO® structure to represent a difficult situation they have faced and discuss positive outcomes that resulted from or in spite of that situation.

Procedures

1. To begin this activity, I like to ask the students if they have ever heard of a bird called a "phoenix." Have them tell you what they know about it. If the students have not heard of it before, you may wish to share a brief story or video about the mythology of the phoenix. After this, introduce them to the phrase "rising like a phoenix from the ashes" and ask them what they think it means.
2. Next, explain that sometimes in life, we might be faced with situations where we feel like we are faced with obstacles that are impossible to overcome or that affect us in significant ways, however, sometimes those difficult situations can actually result in positive outcomes that we could never imagine. Just like the phoenix rising from the ashes, sometimes we can come out of a difficult situation stronger or better than we were before. As an example, I like to share the story of professional surfer Bethany Hamilton, who lost her arm due to a shark attack. Many people thought her career was over and that she would never surf again, but despite what happened, she was able to come back and win a national title in surfing and has her own charitable foundation to support amputees.
3. Ask the students if they can think of any major events that may have been very unfortunate situations, but also resulted in something good happening (e.g. Notre Dame fire and international rebuilding efforts, Tham Luang cave rescue in Thailand).
4. Next, tell the students that they are going to reflect on an event in their own life that may have been very challenging or difficult in some way. Now create a LEGO® structure that represents that event. When everyone has an idea, have them begin building.
5. As the students are building, check in with each student to discuss what they are making and offer support as needed. You may wish to discuss with the students individually what they would like to share with the group to help them prepare for talking about their project as this can be an emotional task for some students as they reflect on challenging events in their lives.

6. When students are done building, have them pause and take a deep breath to help ensure that everyone is calm and feels ready to share about their LEGO® structures and what they represent.
7. Close the session by facilitating a conversation using the discussion questions below.

Discussion Questions

1. What emotions did you experience when this event happened to you?
2. What strategies did you use to help you cope with the situation?
3. Who are people that you can turn to for support when you are faced with a difficult situation?
4. Thinking about the situation that you went through, what positive outcomes have there been that you might consider to be a "phoenix rising from the ashes" moment?
5. What can you do to prepare yourself to handle future situations that come up?

Follow-Up or Extension Activity

- Students will create a picture of a phoenix and keep it as a reminder that they can overcome challenges and difficult situations in life even when it might feel like it is impossible or there is no hope. Students could also include an example of positive self-talk with their art for additional inspiration.

ACTIVITY 4.5

DREAM BUILDERS

Description of Activity

Students will build a structure representing a long-term goal or dream as well as another structure representing a short-term goal that will help them to reach their long-term or "dream" goal.

Learning Objective(s)

- Students will discuss the difference between long and short-term goals.
- Students will identify personal long and short-term goals and represent them through LEGO® structures.

Additional Materials Needed

- Paper
- Markers

Procedures

1. Begin by having the students share an example of a sport or game that they like to play. Ask them to explain what the goal of the game is and how you win. Next, discuss with the students that the final goal may be to win the game, but there are also a lot of things that you or your team need to accomplish before they can achieve the final goal of winning. Explain that these are sometimes referred to as "long-term" and "short-term" goals. At this point, I like to show the students a picture of Mt. Everest, the highest mountain on Earth. Explain to the students that if you are a mountain climber, your long-term goal might be to conquer Mt. Everest, but before you can do that you may need to meet a lot of short-term goals. Next, provide the students with a piece of paper and markers and ask them to come up with a list of all of the short-term goals they can think of that they would need to achieve if they wanted to reach their long-term goal of climbing Mt. Everest. If you have a larger group, you may wish to have them do this with a partner.
2. After the students have had a couple minutes to come up with their list have them share and explain their rationale. Discuss which goals they think are most important.
3. Next, share with the students an example of a personal goal you once had and what steps you took to reach that goal. Discuss how meeting the short-term goals eventually led you to achieving the final long-term goal. Examples could be going to college and earning a degree, making varsity on a sports team, or learning to play an instrument. Be sure to emphasize smaller steps that had to be taken in order to get to the final result, such as learning to master a specific note on the guitar before you are able to play the full song.

4. After this, ask the students to think of a long-term or even a dream goal like becoming a professional athlete. Next, have them think about what short-term goals they would need to accomplish to make reaching that dream goal a reality. You may wish to provide them with a piece of paper to write down their ideas. After the students have had a moment to reflect on this, let them know that they are going to create 2 LEGO® structures today. The first structure will represent the long-term or dream goal, and the second structure will represent a short-term goal that they will need to achieve in order to get to their long-term goal. For example, a student may have a long-term goal of becoming a sushi chef, but before they can ever get to that point, they need short-term goals they can work on now to help them prepare to reach that such as knowing how to make sushi rice properly, identifying fish, or even learning to speak Japanese so they can travel to Japan one day to learn more about sushi. Once the students have their idea, have them begin building their LEGO® structures. If all of the students already stated their dream goals, you might wish to have them focus on building a structure representing their short-term goal. If students have extra time, they can build LEGO® structures to represent multiple short-term goals.
5. As the students are building, check in with each student about what their goal is and what they are making. Offer support as needed. You may also begin to facilitate a discussion using questions 1-2 from the discussion questions below.

Discussion Questions

1. What inspired you to choose your long-term or dream goal?
2. Who is someone you know who has achieved this goal that you look up to or would consider to be a role-model or hero?
3. What do you think is going to be the greatest challenge in achieving your dream goal?
4. How can you handle situations where other people might tell you that your dream is impossible or that you can't do it.
5. What habits do you have or want to develop to help you become successful?

Follow-Up or Extension Activity

- Students will build a staircase structure using LEGO® materials. Have the students discuss how each of the steps on the stairs represents a step they are taking or need to take in order to achieve their goal.

KEYS TO SUCCESS

Description of Activity

Students will create keys using LEGO® materials and discuss different strategies that they have learned over the past several sessions to overcome life's challenges and "unlock" the door to success.

Learning Objective(s)

- Students will identify a significant goal they are working on.
- Students will create a model of a key using LEGO® materials and discuss strategies to help them successfully unlock their potential to reach their goals and persevere through challenges.

Additional Materials Needed

- Paper
- Markers
- *Optional: Keys*

Procedures

1. Begin this activity by asking the students to share if they have ever had an experience where they were locked out of somewhere and did not have a key to get in. Discuss what it feels like to be in that type of situation without a key and how it feels when you are finally able to get in either because you found the key or someone showed up to open the door.
2. Next, explain that throughout the last several sessions, we have been working on a lot of different strategies to help us be successful when faced with difficult circumstances. All of these strategies are "keys" to help us unlock doors that stand between us and success. At this point, take out a large piece of paper and have the students work together to come up with a list of the most important strategies or concepts that they remember discussing in previous sessions. You may wish to title the paper "Keys to Success" and have the students draw a key next to each strategy that they write down.
3. Ask the students to reflect on which strategy or "key" they have found to be most meaningful or helpful for them. Then, let the students know we are going to build keys out of LEGO® materials today. At this point, it is helpful to either have some old keys that you can pass out to the students to hold and look at or to show them some pictures of different keys. To make the activity more fun and interesting, choose a variety of different types of keys (e.g. skeleton keys, magical keys, etc.). Ask the students to imagine what

the keys unlock (e.g. a treasure chest). Next, have the students begin building their LEGO® keys. They can design or decorate their key however they want.

4. As the students are building, check in with each student about what strategy they want their key to represent and what "door" or goal the key will help them unlock. Making a key shape with LEGO® materials may be challenging for some students, so provide support as needed.
5. As the students are building, begin facilitating a conversation with questions 1-2 from the discussion questions below.
6. When the students are done building their keys, have them share which strategy or key to success their LEGO® structure represents.

Discussion Questions

1. What are some ways that you can practice using your "key to success" more often?
2. What door are you trying to unlock, or what goal are you trying to achieve?
3. What treasure or reward awaits you on the other side of the door if you unlock it?
4. What doors or goals require more than one key or strategy to unlock?
5. What keys or strategies do you need on your keychain to unlock the next door?

Follow-Up or Extension Activities

- Students will make a treasure chest out of LEGO® materials. Next, have students write down examples of "treasure" or benefits and rewards that will result from achieving their goals such as gaining confidence, college scholarship opportunities, or traveling. You may wish to have students write down their treasure on yellow construction paper and then cut them out in circles to represent gold coins that they can put in their treasure chest.
- Students will make a "Treasure Map to Success" showing the path they must take and challenges or obstacles in their way that they must overcome to reach the treasure or their long-term goal. This would be designed to look like a pirate map and can have location names that correspond with their goal. For example, a student who wants to pass their upcoming math test might have to travel through the "fraction forest" and defeat the "multiplication monster" before they can reach their goal.

SECTION 5

In this section, you will find activities to support students with building a positive sense of self-esteem through exploring personal qualities, character traits, passions, and successes.

AMAZING ANIMALS

Description of Activity

Students will build a LEGO® sculpture of an animal that they feel has remarkable qualities that they identify with or see in themselves.

Learning Objective(s)

- Students will identify with animals and character traits or qualities they feel those animals represent.
- Students will choose an animal they feel represents positive qualities they see in themselves and create LEGO® sculpture of that animal.

Additional Materials Needed

- Paper
- Markers

Procedures

1. Begin by sharing pictures of different animals and having the students share characteristics or qualities that they think define that animal. For example, for a bear, students may say words like strong, protective, brave, sleepy, or playful. Make a list of all of these character traits on a slightly large piece of butcher paper or on a whiteboard.
2. Next, explain to students that they are going to choose an animal that they think has qualities that they have in themselves. You could also have the students imagine that if they were an animal, what would they be and why. You may wish to provide each student with a piece of paper and have them write down the animal they identify with and some the of the characteristics or qualities they share. For example, a student may decide they would be a cheetah because they are a fast runner, or a student may say they would be a dog because they are very dependable. There can be a lot of variation in the types of character qualities that students choose for this activity and that is okay.
3. After students have chosen their animal, have the students begin building their animals with the LEGO® materials. Many students will need some guidance on how to build their animal out of LEGO® bricks, so it is helpful if you have access to pictures or are able to do an online image search for LEGO® versions of the animal they want to build. This will give students a visual example that they can copy or draw inspiration from as they create their own animals.
4. As the students are building their animals, facilitate a group discussion using questions 1-2 from the discussion questions.

5. When the students are done creating their animals, give each student an opportunity to share their LEGO® creation and which characteristics they feel they have in common with that animal.
6. To close the session, facilitate a conversation using the remaining discussion questions below.

Discussion Questions

1. What is your favorite animal and why?
2. How are you most like this animal?
3. What are some qualities in other students' animals that you also see in yourself?
4. What types of qualities do you want to develop in yourself more?
5. What are some steps you can take to develop those qualities?

Follow-Up or Extension Activity

- Students can build a habitat or a home for their animal. Students can discuss supportive or challenging aspects of their environment around them and how it may affect the kind of character traits their animal has or that they have in real life. For example, a student who built an elephant may describe having a large and supportive family.

ACTIVITY 5.2

SHINING STARS

Description of Activity

Students will create a star using LEGO® materials and discuss the personal qualities that make them "shine" or make them unique.

Learning Objective(s)

- Students will discuss the scientific characteristics of stars and how each star's physical makeup is unique (similar to a snowflake).
- Students will identify characteristics that are unique about them and create a star to represent their uniqueness.

Materials Needed

- Paper
- Pencils

Procedures

1. Begin this activity by talking with the students about what they know about stars in outer space. It may be helpful to find a brief article or video online that talks about unique physical makeup of stars. Discuss how each star is unique and special just like they are.
2. Next, explain that today we are going to make a star using LEGO® materials and discuss things that are unique about each one of us. To get started, have a conversation about the meaning of the word unique. To help illustrate the meaning of this word, you may find it helpful to show the students a picture of a famous person or character and have the students come up with anything they can think of that is unique about them. A famous athlete or a fictional superhero could be suitable for this.
3. Before the students start building their star, give each student a piece of paper and a pencil. Ask them to write down 5 things that are unique about them, or one example for each of the 5 points on the star they will be making. As the students are writing, check in with each student and offer support as needed in coming up with a list of 5 items.
4. After each student has their list completed, it is now time to begin building the stars. Making a star with LEGO® bricks can be a bit tricky, so I recommend that you print off a piece of paper with a star outline on it and have the students try to build their star on top using the paper as a template. You could also find a picture or video online of a star built using LEGO® bricks and have the students copy what they see. The students can build their stars using any colors they prefer.

5. As the students are building their stars, facilitate a discussion using questions 1-2 from the discussion questions below.
6. When the students are finished building their stars, have each student share what they made as well as their list of 5 things that make them unique.
7. Close the session by discussing the remaining discussion questions below.

Discussion Questions

1. Today we learned a little bit about the science of stars. What unique subjects do you like to learn about or know a lot about?
2. What made you interested in that subject or how did you first learn about that?
3. When students shared 5 things that made them unique, did you discover that you actually had something in common with someone else?
4. What are some areas where you want to "shine" but you are still trying to get there?
5. How did it make you feel to share about the things that are special about you?

Follow-Up or Extension Activity

- Using the star template or the actual star, have the students trace the outline of the star with their finger and take a deep breath and exhale each time they go up and down on the lines of the star while saying all the qualities that describe them.

BRICKTASTIC SUPERHEROES

Description of Activity

Students will create themselves as a superhero character using LEGO® materials and discuss which superpowers they would have and why.

Learning Objective(s)

- Students will identify positive character traits of their favorite superheroes.
- Students will create a LEGO® version of themselves as a superhero and discuss their own superpowers or positive character traits.

Additional Materials Needed

- Paper
- Markers
- Pencils

Procedures

1. Begin this activity by having each student share their favorite superhero. Make a list of the characters and discuss their superpowers and what character qualities they have.
2. Next, give each student a piece of paper and have them write down what their name would be if they were a superhero and what powers or characteristics they would have. They could also draw a quick sketch of what their costume would look like. Tell them not to show anyone yet because they don't want to give away their "secret identity." You will use their paper later to do a guessing game with the group, so actually have them keep it a secret and tell them not to peek.
3. Next, tell the students that are going to create a LEGO® model of the superhero selves. You may find it helpful to have a super hero version of yourself already created to share with the group for an example. When everyone is ready, have the students start building their superheroes.
4. As the students are building, check in with each student and have them show you their "secret identity" paper. If students need help developing their character, provide support as necessary. Ideally, the characters should reflect something that is truly unique about each student, so you may have suggestions to help them achieve that. For example, if a student is in gymnastics, that could be reflected in the characters superpowers by making them acrobatic.

5. After checking in with each student, collect their papers being careful not to let others see anyone's secret identity. Have the students finish up building and let them know we are going to play "Guess the Secret Identity."
6. To play the game, let the students know that you are going to read some of the character's superpowers and that they can raise their hand if they have a guess who it might be. Students cannot guess themselves, but they could guess someone else to try to make it trickier for the other students to guess correctly. Once a person's secret identity is guessed, go on to the next paper.
7. After everyone's "secret identity" has been revealed, have each student present their LEGO® brick superhero and facilitate a conversation using the group discussion questions below.

Discussion Questions

1. What superpowers does your character have?
2. How would you use these superpowers to benefit others?
3. What are your character's weaknesses?
4. What superpowers or personal strengths do you have in real life?
5. How do you use your strengths to positively impact the world around you?

Follow-Up or Extension Activity

- Using the characters that the students created, have the students make a comic book of their character helping others or overcoming a challenge. Students can base their story on a real-life situation they faced in the past or are currently facing.

SELF-COMPASSION BUILD-UPS

DESCRIPTION OF ACTIVITY

Students will collaboratively build a tower in which each person shares a statement of self-compassion after they add a brick to the structure.

LEARNING OBJECTIVE(S)

- Students will discuss the meaning of self-compassion.
- Students will demonstrate the use of self-compassion statements.

ADDITIONAL MATERIALS NEEDED

- Paper
- Pencils

PROCEDURES

1. Start this activity by discussing the meaning of the word compassion. Have the students share an example of a time when someone showed compassion toward them or a time when they were compassionate toward someone else.
2. Next, discuss with the students how one of the most important ways we show compassion to others is through the words that we say. When we see someone else is having a rough day or things aren't going well, we will often respond by saying something kind, encouraging, or uplifting to others. Ask the students if they can give an example of a time when someone said something kind or encouraging to them.
3. After this, tell the students you are going to give them some different scenarios and we are going to work together to see if we can come up with compassionate or encouraging statements to say to someone in these situations. Here are some scenarios to read to the students;
   - You see someone trip and drop their art project on the ground.
   - Someone is playing soccer and they miss the game-winning goal.
   - Your friend just got their math test back and they failed it.
4. Now that the students have come up with positive and encouraging statements that they would say to someone else, ask them if this is what they would say to themselves if they were the person making the mistake. Have the students give examples of negative self-talk they might use in those situations.

5. Next, introduce students to the term self-compassion and ask them what they think it means. Tell them that today we are going to practice using self-compassion as a way to build ourselves up when we make a mistake or have a rough day through an activity called self-compassion build ups.
6. Explain that to do this activity, we are going to work together to see how many examples of self-compassion statements we can come up with as a team. Each time we come up with an example we are going to add a brick to our tower and see how tall we can make it. Take turns going around the table and have each person try to think of examples of statements. Sample statements could be "you got this," "you are worth it," or "you will get through this." If a student is having a hard time thinking of an example, offer a scenario and ask them what they could say to themselves in that situation. If you know what a student's interests or hobbies are, you could make the situation about that to try to make it more authentic for the student.
7. After each student has had an opportunity to share 2-3 examples of self-compassion statements and add to the brick tower, close the session by facilitating a conversation using the discussion questions below.

Discussion Questions

1. What makes it easier to show compassion to others than to ourselves?
2. When do you tend to be hardest on yourself or use a lot of negative self-talk?
3. How can you start to show yourself more self-compassion when you make a mistake or things don't go the way you had hoped?
4. How do you think you will feel about yourself if you start to practice more self-compassion?
5. In what ways can you practice self-compassion besides using positive self-talk?

Follow-Up or Extension Activity

- To continue to reinforce the importance of self-compassion, keep the tower that the students built and continue to add to it each session by letting the students share any examples of how they used self-compassion throughout the week. Every week, students will see the tower growing and it will serve as a visual reminder that they can practice self-compassion.

BUILDING YOUR PASSION

Description of Activity

Students will create a LEGO® structure representing an activity that they are passionate about and discuss why they value it and how it has impacted their life.

Learning Objective(s)

- Students will identify an activity that they really enjoy or that has a big role in their life.
- Students will create a LEGO® model to represent that activity and discuss how their participation has had an effect on their character development and self-esteem.

Procedures

1. Begin by sharing an example of your own passion or an activity that you enjoy doing. I suggest that you bring in something physical that you can show and tell the students about to make it more authentic and engaging. For example, if you are a hiker, you could bring your hiking backpack and tell them about all of the different pockets and what gear you bring with you on your hikes. If you are a musician, you could bring your instrument and play a song for them and tell about how you first started learning to play. It really can be anything as long as it is authentically related to an activity that you have a passion for and is practical and safe to bring.
2. Next, take a moment to discuss the meaning of the word passion. In our case, passion refers to a hobby or activity that we are deeply interested in or enjoy doing. Then, give the students an opportunity to share about one of their own passions.
3. Once everyone has shared, explain that today we are going to make a structure with LEGO® materials that represents an activity we are passionate about. Let the students know that they can choose a variety of things to represent what they like and that it is up to them what they want to build. They can be very creative too. You may wish to share a couple of examples to help them develop a better concept of what they can do for this activity. Some examples could include building a paintbrush to represent a passion for art, a cupcake to represent a passion for baking, or a swimming pool to represent a passion for swimming.
4. After the students have decided on the activity they want to represent through their LEGO® structures, have them begin building. As the students are building, check in with each student to see if they need any support and to discuss what they have chosen for the project.
5. As the students are building, facilitate a group conversation using discussion questions 1-2 from the discussion questions.

6. After students are finished, give each student an opportunity to share what they have made, what it represents, and how they came to discover that they have a passion for that activity.
7. Close the session by facilitating a conversation with the remaining discussion questions below.

Discussion Questions

1. Sometimes it is possible to have more than one passion. What are some other passions you thought about building today?
2. What is an activity that you have not done yet, but are passionate about wanting to try or learn more about?
3. What do you like most about the activity you shared today?
4. What challenges are involved in your activity and how do you handle those?
5. How has participating in your activity helped you grow in your character or what lessons have you learned as a result of participating?

Follow-Up or Extension Activity

- After the students have shared their passion, ask them if they would be willing to demonstrate, teach, or bring something for show and tell with the group (with parent permission) to help us learn more about their activity. Showing an interest in what the student enjoys and giving them more opportunities to share their passion with others is a good way to make them feel validated, provide a leadership opportunity, and build their self-esteem.

BUILDING POSITIVE QUALITIES

Description of Activity

Students will create a word using LEGO® bricks to discuss positive qualities that define who they are.

Learning Objective(s)

- Students will identify positive characteristics about themselves.
- Students will choose a word that characterizes who they are using LEGO® materials.

Additional Materials Needed

- Baseplates or Construction Paper
- Notecards
- Markers
- Pencils

Procedures

1. Begin this activity by giving each student a small piece of a paper such as a sticky note or index card and ask them to write down one positive word to describe the counselor or leader. Collect these from the students and read the words out loud. Alternatively, you could make a list together and have the students say the words out loud and you could write them on paper or a whiteboard.

2. After this, talk to the students about how good these words made you feel. Next, have the students come up with positive words to describe each other. To do this, give each student a small piece of paper and have them write their name at the top. The paper will then be passed to the person next to them and will rotate through the circle until it comes back to the owner. Each time a student gets a new paper, have them write down a positive word to describe that person. When each person gets their original paper back, it should have at least a couple of positive words on it such as "helpful," "kind," or "good basketball player." For older students, you might ask them to write more detailed affirmations or more than one word to describe each person.

3. Next, have the students share how it made them feel to receive the positive words. Discuss that while it is nice for other people to describe us in a positive way, it is also important that we think of ourselves in a positive way too.

4. After this, share with the students that today we are going to be building a word that we feel represents us using LEGO® materials. It is helpful to have an example to show students how they can make letters using LEGO® bricks. This can also be done using various

language scripts or characters which means students could choose to build words in different languages for this activity if they choose. For example, a word could be built in Arabic or Japanese. For this activity, ask students to focus on building one word that defines them, but allow them to create multiple words if they finish one word and other students still need more time.

5. As the students are building, check in to see if anyone needs additional support. Creating letters can be a bit tricky, so students may need to see some examples to help them figure out how to best make them. You may wish to have access to online images for examples. Also, check to make sure the students have chosen words to share that are positive.
6. When the students are finished with their words, give each student an opportunity to share their word and give an example of how they display that characteristic or why they chose that particular word.
7. Close the session by facilitating a conversation using the discussion questions below.

Discussion Questions

1. How was it challenging to choose one word for this project?
2. How does the word that you chose match with what others have shared about you?
3. When do you find yourself using negative words to define yourself?
4. How do the words you choose to define yourself affect your self-esteem?
5. How can you develop the habit of using positive words to define who you are?

Follow-Up or Extension Activity

- After students build their words, take a photo of their work and upload it into a document on the computer that can be shared with the students. Using the word as their topic, have the students write about how they demonstrate that characteristic or in what ways that word defines them. You may also want to have students include a picture of themselves in their document. (For a challenge, ask students to take the first letter of their word and write other character words that describe them beginning with the same letter).

COLLABORATION-BASED ACTIVITIES

Overview and Topics

Collaboration-Based activities can be an exciting and effective way to support students with the development of important social-emotional skills in a group setting. Through collaborative building experiences, students can be engaged in authentic and exciting play-based and project-based activities that are designed to appeal to different age-groups and support the development of various social-emotional skills such as:

- Teamwork
- Friendship
- Communication
- Problem-Solving
- Emotion Regulation
- Empathy

Guidelines for Facilitating Collaboration-Based Activities

Collaboration-based activities are designed to promote the development of positive peer interactions and social skills through age-appropriate collaborative or play-based activities. Groups for older students (typically 3rd-8th grade) emphasize project-based and blended learning activities that promote more rigorous practice and application of 21st century skills (Communication, Collaboration, Critical Thinking, Creativity) and integration of technology and academic skills. Groups for younger students (typically Preschool-2nd grade) are focused primarily on developing appropriate play skills, problem-solving, and nurturing friendships through positive shared-experiences.

For collaboration groups, I recommend a more Adlerian approach where the counselor encourages all students to take an active role in the project and be a contributing member of the group. This supports the Adlerian concept of Gemeinschaftsgefühl, or social responsibility, which strengthens each participant's sense of purpose in the group. Depending on the type of group, there may be a variety of different skills that students need to demonstrate in order to be successful. In this case, the facilitator may assume the role of a teacher and model or role play certain skills. This task could also be delegated to students to provide valuable opportunities for leadership, peer-to-peer modeling, and assessment purposes to determine student mastery of different skills.

All of the activities in this book are designed for a typical 30-minute group session following the outline below:

Suggested Outline for a 30-Minute Session

1. Welcome and Group Norms
2. Review Goal
3. Introduce Activity
4. Mini-Lesson
5. Activity Work Time
6. Presentations and Compliments
7. Clean up
8. Self-Assessment

*Note on Saving Projects

It's important to note that there is also a potential challenge awaiting at the end of the session as many students will feel a strong sense of pride in what they built and will ask to save their creations and put them on display. At times, it may be possible to put a few items on a shelf and save them for a little while, but inevitably you will run out of space to keep doing this and you will probably find that you need the pieces to complete projects with other groups. To manage this issue, there are 3 solutions that I have found to be effective:

1. Share with students that building with LEGO® bricks is similar to building a sandcastle on the beach and that it won't last forever. I will typically allow them to put their item on a shelf in the office somewhere to display it and then I will disassemble it at the end of the day.

2. Create a digital portfolio of their work by taking a picture of each of their builds and then printing it for them at the conclusion of the group. Typically students are comfortable with disassembling their projects once you take a picture of it. Actually creating a portfolio and managing pictures of individual student projects is time consuming, so be mindful about whether or not you can commit to this solution.

3. Enforce a rule that everyone must clean up and put all of the materials away once the timer goes off. Some students have a difficult time with transitioning and this can turn into a power struggle on occasion. For students that have a hard time cleaning up and moving on, I usually ask them to leave their pieces on the table so they are not late going back to class. If you know certain students who need more time to transition, it can be helpful to set a timer before the actual clean-up timer to let them know they have 2 minutes left to finish building before everyone is going to put the materials away.

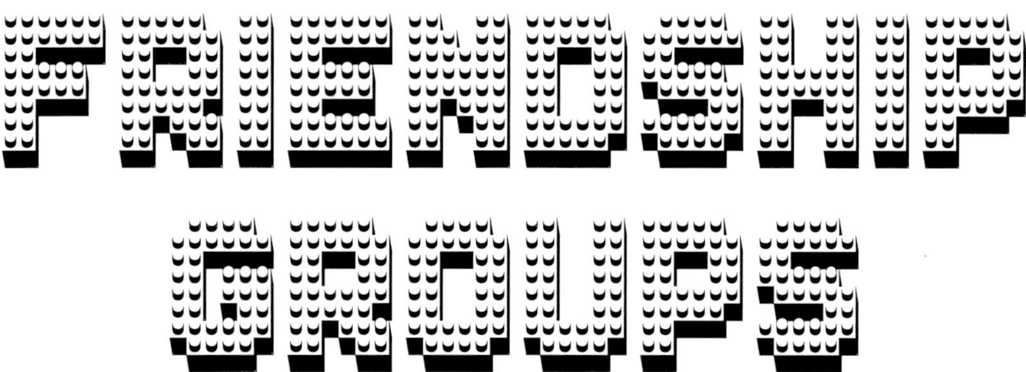

FRIENDSHIP GROUPS

SECTION 6

Friendship activities using Classic LEGO® bricks and Minifigures® provide a collaborative play-based environment in which students can authentically practice and develop social skills with opportunities for appropriate modeling, scaffolding, coaching, and feedback. The actual project the students build is secondary and can be either determined by the facilitator or left up to the participants to decide. The act of building together is intended to encourage active participation and interaction and provides an authentic environment in which the counselor/leader may offer social and emotional skills coaching, reinforcement, and feedback. These groups are especially effective and engaging for younger students who often need support with fundamental play and friendship skills, or for older students who may be kinesthetically oriented and would benefit from a hands-on approach to building social skills.

Each group session begins with a "mini-lesson" on a particular social-emotional skill that students will be asked to focus on practicing or demonstrating during the activity for that session. Typically, this mini-lesson should be about 5 minutes in length but could take longer at times depending on the needs of the students. I have included 6 example mini-lessons that you can use in this section. You may develop your own mini lessons around other topics or skills based on the needs of the participants. These lessons provide the foundation for both themed group sessions as these are the primary social-emotional skills students will be working on developing.

When you first begin implementing a brick-based program, you likely will not have many LEGO® Minifigure characters. Not to worry, there are literally thousands of things you can build with LEGO® bricks that you could use for your group that do not require LEGO® Minifigure(s). A quick internet search will provide access to many fun project ideas. Additionally, specific instructions for different projects using Classic LEGO® bricks are available on the official LEGO® website. Here is a list of 10 suggestions that are generally simple to implement with a basic set of materials:

1. House
2. Animals
3. Airplane
4. Restaurant
5. Store
6. Park
7. Boat
8. Flower
9. Food
10. Robot

Having a collection of LEGO® Minifigure(s) characters at your disposal opens up even more possibilities and provides opportunities to engage students on a deeper level and perhaps connect more with their personal interests. For example, if you are working with a group of students who love super- heroes, providing an opportunity to participate in a group based on this particular theme could be very exciting. Themed groups can be offered with a limited number of characters, but as your collection grows, you will be able to offer a wider variety of activities to keep participants engaged throughout the duration of a multi-week group. For example, if you were offering a superhero group and have access to multiple characters, you could select different superhero "team ups" for each session to help keep it fun and interesting. Again, the characters and the projects offered are intended to increase student engagement and participation and encourage an active collaborative play environment in which the counselor can support student social-emotional growth.

Below is a description of some sample themed groups you could offer depending on what types of LEGO® Minifigure(s) characters you have access to, along with suggested building projects.

- **Community Helpers -** This group provides a valuable opportunity for students to learn about community helpers and the importance of making a difference for others. Access to characters representing a variety of professional roles may also provide a fun way to explore different careers. Projects could include a fire station, zoo, post office, recycling center, market, library, or other community locations.
- **Superheroes -** This group utilizes popular superhero characters and provides a great opportunity for students to explore the qualities of being a superhero, personal strengths, and how they can use their own "superpowers" to help others. If characters come with weapons, these can be removed to make them more appropriate for your setting. Projects might include the superhero bases, vehicles, or setting up scenes where the superheroes can help someone in need.
- **Storybook Adventures –** This group can feature a general variety of characters such as pirates, knights, or other fantasy characters. Projects could include making a pirate ship, castle, haunted house, or aliens from outer space. Utilizing common characters and themes found in stories also creates an opportunity to integrate books and bibliotherapy activities with the building sessions.

These are just a few examples of themes that could potentially be used depending on what resources and characters you have access to. As you plan what types of activities you want to include in your sessions, make sure to consider if the thematic elements related to different characters or sets are a good fit or appropriate for your setting and goals. For example, some themes based on popular movies might contain weapons or other elements that you may want to take into consideration. With some creativity, you could remove components that you do not feel are appropriate for your setting or develop modified projects that are fun and interesting. For example, in a school setting, I may not want students creating a movie spaceship with lots of lasers and weapons, but we could still create a spaceship and utilize popular characters in a school appropriate manner. Remember, the theme is primarily to attract the interest and engagement of the students that will encourage an authentic play-based context for them to develop social-emotional skills.

SHARING IDEAS, LISTENING, AND MAKING A PLAN TOGETHER

Description of Activity

Students will practice communication skills through taking turns talking, listening, and making a plan together to build a tower using 2 colors.

Learning Objective(s)

- Students will demonstrate sharing ideas and listening in a respectful way.
- Students will collaborate to make a plan for building a LEGO® structure.

Procedures

1. To begin this mini-lesson, ask students why they think it is important to listen to others (e.g. it is respectful, to understand them, to show you care, etc.). You may wish to write down their ideas on a piece of paper or a whiteboard. Discuss if they have ever had an experience where they felt like someone was not listening to them and how that made them feel.
2. Next, share that today we will be doing a brief activity where they will have to work together to make a tower. Before they can start building though, each student will need to respectfully share an idea for how to build the tower, while the other student demonstrates respectful listening. At this point, you may want to ask the students to list traits of each of these, such as being a good listener by showing interest and focusing on what the other person is saying, and sharing ideas respectfully by not being demanding. These ideas should be written down on a piece of paper or whiteboard as the students share them. Let the student know that this list is now a tool that can be utilized as a checklist of success criteria to refer back to later so they can self-assess if they are using the skills or behaviors they identified.
3. After this, explain that after each person has a chance to share, they will need to agree on a plan to build their tower. You may wish to provide students with a piece of paper and something to write or draw their plan with.
4. Next, pass out the materials for students to build their tower with their partner. Each student should receive about 5-10 LEGO® bricks of a single color, which means each pair will have to decide how to build their tower using 2 colors. Students could choose to alternate their colors or develop a unique pattern.
5. Have the students decide who will be sharing their idea first and begin their conversation. As they are discussing their ideas and making their plan, monitor to see that students are using appropriate social-emotional skills and demonstrating the items on the checklist the students generated. Provide support as needed.

6. When the students have finished, provide each pair an opportunity to share what they made and how well they think they used the skills on the checklist by using a self-assessment strategy such as showing a thumbs up, thumbs sideways, or thumbs down to indicate their comfort level with each of the skills.
7. Discuss the questions below and let students know that you would like them to focus on sharing ideas respectfully, listening respectfully, and making a plan together when they do the next building project (this project will be based on whatever the theme is for the group, such as Community Helpers or Superheroes).

Discussion Questions

1. How did it feel to have your partner listen to you and not interrupt?
2. How was it for you to listen to your partner's ideas after they respectfully listened to your ideas?
3. How was your plan affected by respectfully speaking and listening to each other?
4. If you could pick one item from our checklist today as a goal to really focus on as we do our next activity, which one would you like to choose?
5. What strategies will you use to help you stay focused on your goal?

Follow-Up or Extension Activity

- If building a tower with 2 colors is too simple of a task for your students, you can increase the complexity by giving the students additional colors or special LEGO® pieces such as windows or doors that must be incorporated into their plan.

SHARING, TRADING, AND TAKING TURNS

Description of Activity

In this activity, students will practice using skills to share, trade, or take turns with various LEGO® items to resolve or prevent conflicts.

Learning Objective(s)

- Students will discuss respectful words to use when offering to share, trade, or take turns.
- Students will demonstrate using these strategies to resolve or prevent conflicts.

Procedures

1. Begin this activity by asking the students if they have ever been in a situation where someone was not playing in a fair way. Ask them to describe some things that made it unfair (e.g. not sharing, not letting others have a turn, taking something without asking). Make a list of these items on a piece of paper or whiteboard.
2. Let the students know that today we are going to focus on using 3 strategies, sharing, trading, and taking turns, to help us play and work together in a fair way. Have the students discuss examples of respectful language they could use for each of the 3 strategies and examples for when they might use those strategies. Write these ideas down by making a column for each strategy. You may wish to provide students with a sentence starter for each strategy such as "Is it okay if we use A together?," "Would you like to trade A for B?," or "Can I please have a turn with A? Write each of these example phrases on the paper or whiteboard and let the students know that we will be using this visual as a tool to help us remember how to use our strategies to play fairly.
3. Next, have the students practice each of these phrases by offering some sample scenarios with a couple of LEGO® Minifigure(s) or other LEGO® creations. For example, if you have two different characters, you can ask the students to give examples of what they would say if they wanted to share and play together, if they wanted to trade characters, or if they wanted to ask to have a turn with one of the characters. If you do not have LEGO® Minifigure(s) to demonstrate with, you could still illustrate and have the students demonstrate the different strategies using LEGO® bricks of different colors (i.e. Would you like to trade the green brick for the yellow brick?)
4. After going through a scenario for each of the strategies as a whole group, let the students know that they are going to have the opportunity to work with a partner to practice using each of the three skills or questions from the poster we created.
5. To do this activity, provide each student with a LEGO® Minifigure or single LEGO® brick of different colors. Have the students take turns demonstrating each of the 3 strategies. This is also a good opportunity to remind students to use their strategies for respectful speaking and listening that they practiced in the previous session.

6. As the students are practicing each of the three strategies, monitor to see that students are using the strategies appropriately and will provide support as needed.

7. When the students have had a turn to use all 3 strategies, have them look at the visual with the 3 strategies and do a self-assessment of how well they did on each strategy such as holding up a 1, 2, or 3 to rate their comfort level for using each. Discuss the questions below and let students know that you would like them to focus on using each of these 3 strategies as they are completing the next building project (based on the theme of the group).

Discussion Questions

1. How did it make you feel when your partner asked you respectfully to share, trade, or take turns?

2. If you think someone wants to have a turn or share something, what is the best way to handle that type of situation?

3. If someone is willing to share, trade, or take turns, how does that make you feel?

4. If you could pick one item from our checklist today as a goal to really focus on as we do our next activity, which one would you like to choose?

5. What strategies will you use to help you stay focused on your goal?

Follow-Up or Extension Activity

- As the students are working on their main activity for that session, have them keep track of how often someone uses one of the 3 strategies (share, trade, or take turns) by making a tally mark on a sticky note. This can be set up easily by having the students make 3 columns on their paper and placing the letters S, T, and TT at the top of each column as abbreviations for each of the strategies. At the end of the group session, students can total up their "points" and also identify which strategy they used the most and which one they can work on more. You could also use this same strategy to have students individually track their own progress in using one of the specific goals that they identified as a goal in discussion question 4 above.

OFFERING AND ASKING FOR HELP

Description of Activity

Students will practice respecting boundaries when offering help and being polite and confident in asking for help when needed.

Learning Objective(s)

- Students will discuss and demonstrate respectful ways to offer help and how to respectfully accept or decline help.
- Students will discuss and demonstrate how to be polite and confident asking for help when needed.

Procedures

1. Begin this activity by discussing if they have ever had a situation where someone tried to do something for them, but you didn't want their help. Ask them to share what that felt like and how they handled that situation. Make a list of feelings and potential solutions on a piece of paper or whiteboard.
2. Next, discuss with the students that when we are working on LEGO® projects together we often may want to help others or we may need to ask for help. Today we are going to practice doing that respectfully and recognizing when someone wants or does not want help. To model these skills, ask one of the students to volunteer to be your partner for a demonstration. Start by modeling unwanted or uninvited help. To do this, give the student some LEGO® materials and ask them to start building something. Wait a few seconds and then demonstrate offering unwanted help by saying things like "I know how to do that, I can help you fix that, give it to me," and then physically taking over the LEGO® project. Ask the students how they think that situation would make them feel and what happened that caused those feelings. Now, have the students explain how you could have offered help in a more respectful way. Make a list of the ideas the students share (e.g. asking first, not touching their project, respecting their personal space). You may wish to make 2 columns on your paper and label one side "offering help" and the other side "asking for help." Then, ask the students what they could say if they want to either accept or decline the offer to help (e.g. "yes, please" or "no, thank you"). If you feel there is a need, you could also talk with the students about making sure that if someone declines their help, that you should be careful about asking again or insisting that they let you help as this might upset them. The students may ask what to do if the situation is a problem where the other person is not sharing or letting them be part of the group. Let them know that we will discuss problem-solving situations like that for our mini-lesson in the next session.
3. After you have talked about offering help, now discuss what to do if you want to ask for help. Ask the students if they have ever been in a situation where they needed help,

but had a hard time asking for some reason (scared, didn't want others to think they couldn't do it, embarrassed). Ask the students, "What was the outcome of not asking for help?" Discuss why it is important to ask for help when needed and what strategies we can use to help us feel more confident about speaking up (e.g. positive self-talk, deep breathing, strong and respectful voice). Write these ideas and strategies down in the "asking for help" column on your paper or the whiteboard. To model using the skill of asking for help, have another student volunteer to help you demonstrate. For this demonstration, begin building something with LEGO® materials while the other student sits next to them. After a few seconds, pretend to get frustrated and act like something is really hard to put together. Then take a deep breath to calm down and quietly say to yourself, "This is really difficult to make, maybe I can ask a friend to help me." Before asking for help, you could also pretend to be a little nervous and then say to yourself, "I can do this," and then turn to the student and respectfully ask them to help you with the project by saying, "Could you please help me with this?" Ask the students to look at the list they made and identify which strategies you demonstrated.

4. At this point, have the students turn to a partner and practice offering help by asking, "Would you like me to help you with that?" and then responding appropriately. Make sure each student has a turn. Then have them turn to a new partner and practice asking for help by saying, "Could you please help me with this?"
5. When the students have finished, have them look at the skills on the checklist and do a self-assessment.
6. Discuss the questions below and let students know that you would like them to focus on offering help respectfully, respecting someone's answer if they decline help, and using their strategies such as positive self-talk or deep breathing to be confident in asking for help as they work on the next building project (the project will depend on the theme for the group).

Discussion Questions

1. How does it feel if someone tries to help you when you don't want help?
2. How can you decline in a polite way if someone wants to help you?
3. If someone asks you to help them, but you are busy, what is a polite way to let them know you are not able to help right now?
4. If you could pick one item from our checklist today as a goal to really focus on as we do our next activity, which one would you like to choose?
5. What strategies will you use to help you stay focused on your goal?

Follow-Up or Extension Activity

- As they are working, test the students on their skills by offering help and asking for help in both positive and negative ways to let them demonstrate their responses.

ACTIVITY 6.4

HANDLING DISAGREEMENT AND CONFLICT

Description of Activity

Students will practice using conflict resolution skills to handle common disagreements or conflicts that may come up as they are working with others.

Learning Objective(s)

- Students will identify common problems that may occur when working on a LEGO® project with another student.
- Students will discuss and demonstrate safe and respectful strategies to handle various problem situations.

Procedures

1. Begin by asking the students if they have ever had a conflict come up while they were working on a LEGO® project. Ask the students to share examples, but to do so without naming anyone so that people do not get their feelings hurt or feel embarrassed about something you share. To help them with this, you may wish to provide them with a sentence starter such as "one time I was working with a partner and…". Write down examples of conflicts on a piece of paper or whiteboard. Examples could include not sharing LEGO® materials, not letting others help with the project, taking someone else's LEGO® pieces without asking, or making fun of something someone made.
2. Next, ask the students to share any strategies they used that were helpful (e.g. asking them to please stop, sharing, calming down) or not helpful (e.g. yelling, being rude, refusing to work together) in solving the problem. Write down their ideas. You may wish to create 2 columns titled "helpful" and "not helpful." Remind students that when we are sharing, we want to be serious about our strategies and not get silly. When students see the phrase "not helpful," some students may try to use this as an opportunity to try to be funny or get a reaction by thinking of outlandish or inappropriate examples of things that are not helpful. For example, they might say they solved the problem by punching someone or something else that maybe didn't actually happen. Once your list is complete, remind students that we will be using this visual as a checklist to help us remember to use safe and respectful problem-solving strategies.
3. Next, let the students know that we are going to practice using a couple of the strategies by pretending to have a problem with a partner. To do this, start by choosing one of the common problems that the students identified earlier. If you know there is an issue that has been occurring more frequently, you may wish to address that directly with the students and let them know that you feel that is one that we need to work on together. If you don't have a specific type of problem you want to work on, select one of the students to choose a situation that they want to practice resolving.

4. Begin by letting the students know you are going to model for them by role playing the situation with a partner and then they will each have an opportunity to practice the same situation. The problem you choose to role play will depend on your group, but an example could be if someone took your LEGO® piece and you are arguing over who had it first. To model this, pretend to be building something with a pile of LEGO® materials and have a student take one of the pieces in front of you. Pretend to get really frustrated, then pause and have the students identify what the problem was and how they think you are feeling. Ask the students what they think you should do before you try to solve the problem if you are feeling really frustrated (e.g. take a deep breath, use a calm-down strategy). Model the calm down strategy and say, "I'm calm now, but what should I do next?" and have the students offer suggestions to coach you through solving the problem. Follow the prompting of the students, but intentionally do something that is not helpful for solving the problem so that the students will have to correct you. For example, the students may tell you to "ask if you can have your piece back." Follow what the students said, but perhaps use a sarcastic tone of voice or say it while crossing your arms. Be sure to exaggerate and do it in a playful way so the students know you are pretending. This will give the students a chance to correct you and be more specific about how to solve the problem in a helpful way. After this, provide any needed materials and have each of the students role play the same situation and an appropriate and respectful solution with a partner.

5. As the students are practicing their problem-solving strategies, monitor to ensure that students are using the strategies from the checklist and demonstrating appropriate social-emotional skills. Provide support as needed. You may wish to have the students role play more than one problem-solving scenario and strategy to ensure competency.

6. When the students have finished, provide each student an opportunity to share which strategy they used and how well they think they used the skills on the checklist.

7. Discuss the questions below and let students know that you would like them to focus on using safe and respectful problem-solving strategies if needed when they do the next building project (this project will be based on the group theme).

Discussion Questions

1. Why it is important to know how to solve problems respectfully?
2. What role does managing your emotions play in helping you solve problems?
3. How does it feel if someone solves a problem with you in a respectful way?
4. If you could pick one item from our checklist today as a goal to really focus on as we do our next activity, which one would you like to choose?
5. What strategies will you use to help you stay focused on your goal?

Follow-Up or Extension Activity

- As they are working, playfully create small conflicts with the students to have them demonstrate using their problem-solving strategies (e.g. take their LEGO® Minifigure).

RESPECTING DIFFERENT PERSPECTIVES

Description of Activity

Students will learn to respect differences and compromise while collaborating with a partner to build a LEGO® structure using 2 different sets of directions.

Learning Objective(s)

- Students will discuss and demonstrate strategies to understand and show respect when others have an idea or perspective different from their own.
- Students will discuss and demonstrate strategies to compromise and work together.

Procedures

1. Begin this activity by discussing with the students if they have ever had a situation where they had a hard time agreeing with someone. Ask them to share some examples and discuss what things make it hard to understand or agree with someone else's perspective. Ask the students to define what the word "perspective" means. To help illustrate how others can have different perspectives, I like to share some examples of ambiguous images or reversible figures. A very famous one of these images looks like a duck when looked at from one perspective, and like a rabbit from another perspective. Do an online search and pull up a couple of these images to look at with the students and have them tell you what they see. Discuss how the images can be looked at different ways to see different things and that both perspectives are correct. Again, go back to the question of why it can be hard to understand someone else's perspective and use a piece of paper or whiteboard to write down the students' ideas (e.g. not able to see what they are looking at, too focused on my own ideas, not paying attention to details). Also discuss strategies to more effectively understand different perspectives and write these ideas down as well (e.g. listening, empathy, patience).
2. Next, let the students know that they are going to be playing a game called "Puzzle Tower" in which they are going to be asked to build a tower with a partner, but they are each going to have a different set of directions or perspective on how to build it. Together, they will have to figure out how to compromise to create a structure that includes and respects both perspectives. As an example, students might be asked to build a tower with 10 bricks. Student A receives a card that says the tower must include "at least 1 red and 3 blue bricks, but no green bricks." Student B receives a card that says the tower must include "exactly 2 red and 3 white bricks." The challenge is that the students have to try to build the tower together, but they cannot tell the other person what their directions are (if it proves to be too difficult, you can let them share their directions to help them try to figure it out). If you want to make it more challenging for older students, you can make the rule of the game that they can't talk at all and you can increase the number of bricks or colors to make it more complex. To complete the challenge, students will have

to develop strategies such as sorting out pieces by color and number on the table or using hand gestures to communicate. It may be helpful to demonstrate this activity for the students by doing a simple example such as a tower with only 5 bricks. Student A will receive a card that says "at least 1 black and 1 green brick, but no red bricks." Student B will receive a card that says "exactly 1 blue brick." Together, both partners will know at least 3 of the bricks for the puzzle. Student B does not know that the tower cannot have red bricks, so if he tries to add a red brick, Student A will gesture to stop him from adding it to the tower. Likewise, Student A does not know that the tower can only have exactly 1 blue brick, so if he tries to add a second blue brick, Student B will try to stop him. Through paying attention to their partner's responses, the students will be able to determine which bricks do not belong in the tower and by process of elimination figure out how to compromise or agree on which bricks they are allowed to use to build it. There can also be multiple correct solutions to the puzzle.

3. This activity may sound confusing as you read it, but it will make more sense once you actually do it with the students. To set up the activity, give each student a card with 1-3 different conditions or rules on it and the number or bricks and the colors they are allowed or not allowed to use. You can use the example shared above or create your own. Use terms such as "exactly," "at least," "no more than," or "none" to describe the number of each color of brick allowed for the puzzle tower. This activity can prove to be very challenging for some students as it does require some logical and numerical puzzle solving ability, however, remember that the purpose of the activity is not to see who can solve the puzzle, but to have students experience the challenge of attempting to work together respectfully with someone who has a different perspective and hopefully find a way to reach a compromise or agreement. You may modify the game to make it easier by reducing the number of bricks for the puzzle tower to as low as 3 or by having students work with in teams to figure out the puzzle if needed.

4. When the students understand the directions and are ready to attempt the activity, refer back to the list of items they created earlier about ways they can try to be understanding of another's perspective. Let them know the activity may be challenging, but if they focus, have patience, and pay attention to their partner, they will have a better chance at solving the puzzle. Give each student a notecard or sticky note with their rules on it, along with a small tub or pile of LEGO® bricks. Since this game is intended for a mini-lesson, you may wish to set a time limit such as 2 minutes. If the students are really engaged and the activity is valuable, you could extend it.

5. As the students are working on the puzzle, monitor to see if students are attempting to use the skills they identified to help them understand their partner's perspective and provide support as needed. This activity may be very frustrating for some students and you may also need to reinforce student use of calm-down strategies or join in to help them solve the puzzle if they are stuck.

6. When the students are finished or time is up, let the students share what they made and any challenges they experienced while building.

7. Discuss the questions on the next page and let students know that you would like them to focus on respecting others' perspectives and working together to find compromises or ways to agree as they work on the next building project (this project will be based on the group theme).

Discussion Questions

1. How did it feel when your partner did not understand your perspective on how to build the tower?
2. What was the most difficult aspect of doing the puzzle tower game?
3. What strategy helped you the most during the game?
4. If you could pick one item from the checklist today as a goal to really focus on as you do your next activity, which one would you like to choose?
5. What strategies will you use to help you stay focused on your goal?

Follow-Up or Extension Activity

- If students enjoyed playing "Puzzle Tower" or want a bigger challenge, you can also attempt to play this game as whole group by creating a larger tower and having multiple perspectives or sets of directions that must be considered to come up with a correct answer. For example, if you have a group of 4, they could attempt to build a tower with 20 bricks and 4 different sets of directions.

GIVING AND RECEIVING COMPLIMENTS

Description of Activity

Students will practice giving and receiving compliments as a way to acknowledge others and demonstrate kindness.

Learning Objective(s)

- Students will discuss and demonstrate different types of compliments.
- Students will discuss and demonstrate how to receive a compliment.

Procedures

1. Begin this activity by discussing what the word compliment means. Have the students share examples of times when they received a compliment. Also, ask the students to share how it felt to receive a compliment and make a list of their responses on a piece of paper or whiteboard.

2. Next, tell the students we are going to play a game called "Compliment Challenge" where the challenge is to try to think of as many compliments as possible. To start, choose a famous person that the students all know such as an athlete or maybe a teacher that the students all know well. Have the students create a list of as many compliments as they can think of for that person in 1 minute. The compliments can be related to anything such as their character traits, things they are good at, or something they do that you appreciate. Students will likely think of examples that relate to a person's appearance, which is fine, but it is good to encourage students to also try to think of compliments that do not relate to how someone looks. As they share their compliments, write down as many as possible on a piece of paper or on a whiteboard.

3. As a group, have the students read the list of compliments and discuss what types of things were complimented on the most and what other types of compliments could be given. Besides compliments about appearance, two other main categories of compliments that I like to discuss with students are character and action. Character compliments relate to someone's personal qualities such as being kind or honest, and action compliments relate to things a person does, such as playing well in a basketball game or learning another language. If the students did not think of many compliments from one of these 3 categories, discuss a couple of examples and add them to the list.

4. Next, let the students know they are going to practice giving compliments to one another, but before that, they are also going to talk about how to receive a compliment. Discuss with the students what they think the best way to receive a compliment is and if there is something they think they should avoid doing also. You may wish to create a list with 2 columns. Title one side "Do" and the other side "Don't" for things the students think you should and should not do when receiving a compliment. On the "Do" side, students may

come up with ideas such as "say thank you," "smile," "tell them how you feel," or "give them a compliment back." On the "Don't" side, they may come up with "don't brag" or "don't put yourself down." The "Don't" side is usually more challenging, so you may want to provide examples of ways people can deflect or reject compliments. I like to use the analogy that compliments are like a gift and we would not want to reject a gift or make it seem like it is not appreciated. For example, if someone says "wow, you are really good at drawing," saying "oh, I'm not that good" to try to be humble actually devalues the compliment and may make others feel rejected.

5. After this, give the students some example compliments and discuss as a group how you could receive the compliment in a positive way using the "Do" side of their list as a guide. For example, you can use the compliment "wow, you are really good at drawing" again, but this time have the students come up with a better way to respond, such as "Thanks, I really appreciate that!" Once the students have discussed a couple of examples, let them know that they are going to do a brief activity using LEGO® bricks with a partner and at the end, they will be asked to think of a compliment for their partner, and they will also get to practice receiving a compliment.
6. For the next activity, explain to students that they will have 1 minute to work with their partner to build an animal out of LEGO® materials. Instruct the students to reflect while they are working together on something positive they could compliment their partner on that is related to the activity, such as "I really liked your idea for building an elephant" or "I thought it was very kind of you to help me find the piece I wanted." Provide students with LEGO® materials and have them begin building. Have them stop after one minute and have each person demonstrate giving and receiving a compliment. Ask the students to share how the compliment made them feel and have them self-assess their comfort level with giving and receiving compliments.
7. Discuss the questions below and let students know that you would like them to focus on giving and receiving compliments when they do the next building project (this project will be based on the group theme).

Discussion Questions

1. How does giving compliments make a positive difference for others?
2. Who is someone that you would like to give a compliment to?
3. How can we develop the habit of giving compliments more often?
4. If you could pick one item from our checklist today as a goal to really focus on as we do our next activity, which one would you like to choose?
5. What strategies will you use to help you stay focused on your goal?

Follow-Up or Extension Activity

- After practicing compliment giving, students will create compliment cards to give others as a way to show kindness. Students could also write a compliment card to themselves as a way to practice self-compassion and develop a positive self-image.

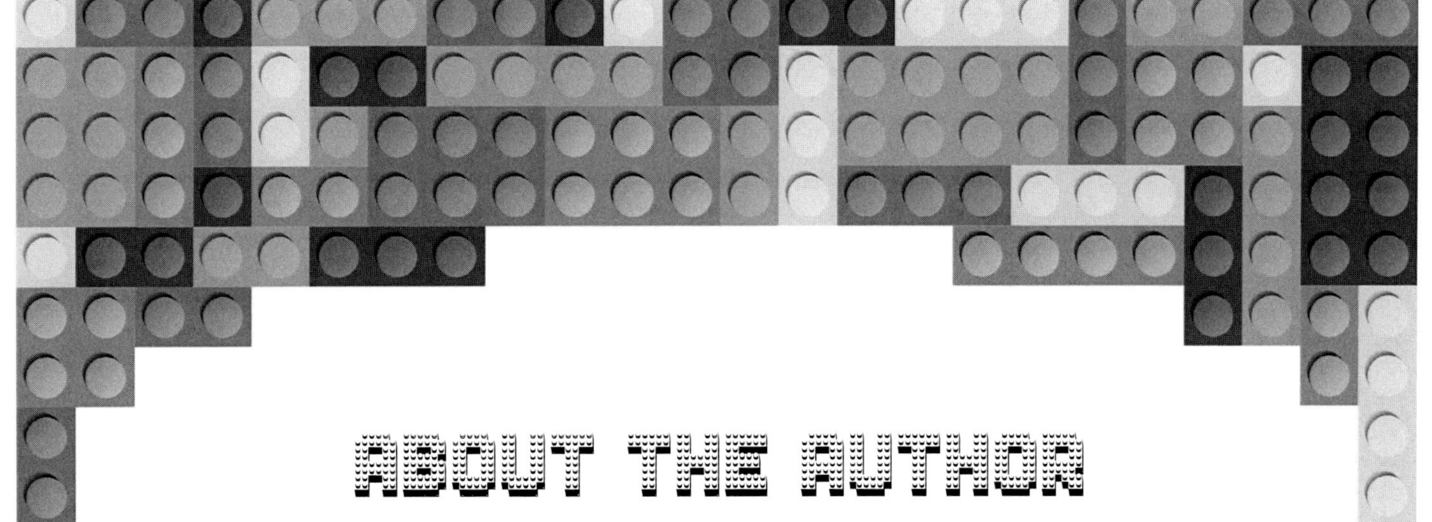

ABOUT THE AUTHOR

Derek Tulluck is a school counselor in the Seattle area in the Enumclaw School District and also teaches a variety of courses at City University of Seattle in the Professional School Counseling graduate degree program. He is a National Board Certified Teacher and completed his M.Ed. in Guidance and Counseling from City University of Seattle, and his BA in Linguistics from Western Washington University. Derek is passionate about incorporating play-based learning strategies and loves using LEGO® materials in his work as a school counselor. Outside of school counseling, Derek is also a black belt in Brazilian Jiu-Jitsu, enjoys traveling, and learning Japanese. Derek lives in Enumclaw, WA with his wife Aya and their 2 children, Walter and Eliana.

Stay connected with the author online by visiting www.brickcounselor.com!

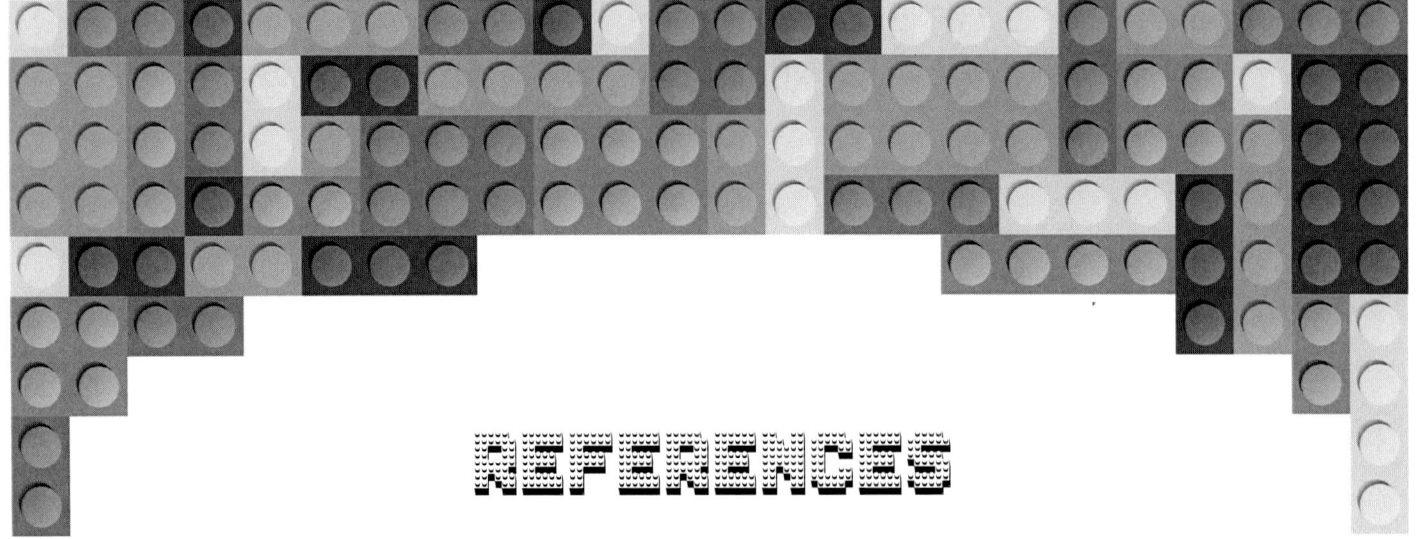

REFERENCES

Gray, P. (2011) The Decline of Play and the Rise of Psychopathology in Children and Adolescents. American Journal of Play, 3, 443-463

Zosh, J. N., Hopkins, E., Jensen, H., Liu, C., Neale, D., Hirsh-Pasek, K., ... Whitebread, D. (2017). Learning through play: a review of the evidence. Billund Denmark: LEGO Foundation.

Stopping Automatic Negative Thoughts (ANTs). (2019, March 14). Retrieved November 1, 2019, from https://www.amenclinics.com/blog/number-one-habit-develop-order-feel-positive/.

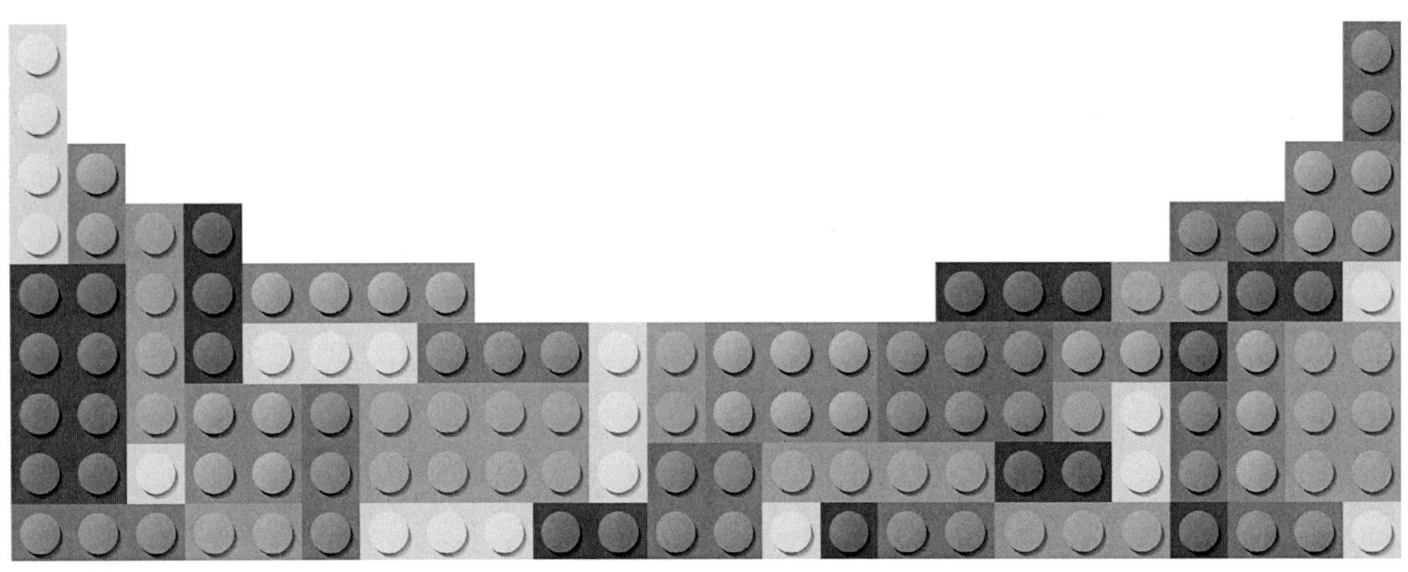